RACHEL SUMMERS

WILD LENT

DISCOVERING GOD THROUGH CREATION

kevin **mayhew**

kevin
mayhew

First published in Great Britain in 2017 by Kevin Mayhew Ltd
Buxhall, Stowmarket, Suffolk IP14 3BW
Tel: +44 (0) 1449 737978 Fax: +44 (0) 1449 737834
E-mail: info@kevinmayhew.com

www.kevinmayhew.com

9 8 7 6 5 4 3 2 1 0

ISBN 978 1 84867 935 1
Catalogue No. 1501572

Cover design by Rob Mortonson
© Images used under licence from Shutterstock Inc.
Typeset by Rob Mortonson
Printed and bound in Great Britain

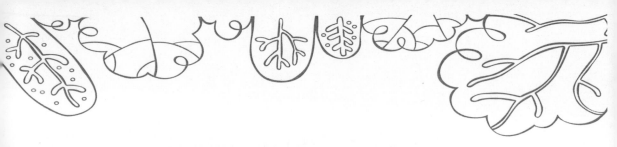

IN PRAISE OF WILD LENT

Lent is a time for us all to reconnect with the divine and this book will be a great tool to help you do that. Take the time to engage with these activities to help you reconnect with the natural world around and deepen your faith in the glorious creator who has made our world a wonderful place to be.

Nikki McKnight, a Forest School Practitioner from WildTree Learning
www.wildtreelearning.co.uk

What a book! Jam-packed full of activities and ideas. Whether you want to briefly dip your little toe into nature, or completely immerse yourself into our wild world by jumping right in, cannonball style, there is something to make everyone learn, remember and smile.

Faye Williams, Forest School Practitioner

There is so much joy and thoughtfulness in these pages.This book provides a wonderful incentive for people of all ages to get out into nature and deepen their connection with the natural world.

Gail Doggett, Mum of two boys, aged 2 and 5

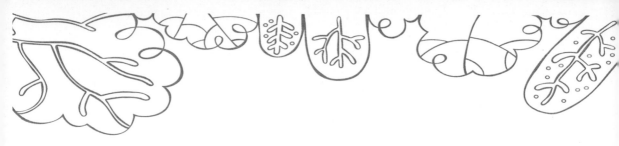

IN PRAISE OF WILD LENT
CONTINUED

It's not easy to be in the moment with my kid – with the many other distractions for both of us. This book makes it deliciously possible, through clearly described actions which we both end up learning from. Connections are made with each other and nature!

Rebecca Tully

Lent is a key time in the Christian calendar and indeed, the seasons of the planet. It's a time when we re-evaluate, after the celebrations and indulgences of the Christmas season; we reconnect again with an earth in waiting. It's a time when things can appear dark, with the year's hopes and plans looming in front of us, as yet unrealised. This book does not hide from the struggles of the season. On the contrary, it faces them head-on, but in a way which is full of hope, action and fun! It is full of activities and reflections that are not just for children but which clearly grow from a deep understanding of the young. Put your wellies on, wrap up warm and give it a go!

Mark Berry, Community Mission Mobiliser, Church Mission Society

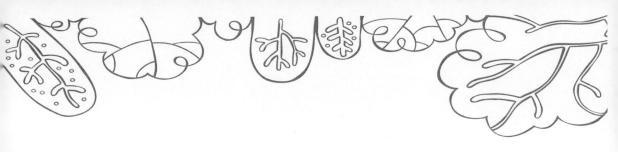

CONTENTS

Short and easy things to make and do

Even shorter and easier things to do

Things to do in the early morning

Things to do on the move

ABOUT THE AUTHOR

Rachel lives in a vicarage in East London with her husband, their five kids, and a veritable menagerie of pets. She loves her corner of the urban wild, and the fact that within a few minutes she can be surrounded by the multicultural busyness of the market, awed by the wide expanse of the marshes, or enclosed amongst the ancient trees of Epping Forest.

A teacher by trade, and daughter of the highly successful author, Susan Sayers, Rachel moved from teaching in primary schools, through doing work one-to-one with excluded teens, to retraining as a forest school practitioner. She now delivers forest school sessions to nurseries, schools, and the general public. Although she never quite manages to scrub the mud off her hands, Rachel believes she has the best job in the world.

Sharing the magic of all things slimy and interesting, watching the seasons shift and the weather change, finding the beauty in the commonplace and insignificant, holding space for others to explore: these are some of the things which get Rachel excited. She gives thanks for the people, communities and world that God has given her to live in and be a part of, and takes delight in sharing that joy with others.

 @wildworshipuk   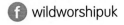 wildworshipuk

WHY WILD LENT?

Lent is a funny old season. Because Easter is a movable feast, linked to the phases of the moon, Lent can come early or late. Sometimes Lent occupies that dark, damp and uncomfortable, grey and sludge green end of winter. Sometimes it's a late Lent, and the world is brightening up before we start. Whenever it comes though, it is a season of movement, marking and tracking a shift between the dark days of winter through the equinox to spring.

With the first proper warm days of the year, shops and adverts spring into life offering us a life full of smiles set against a blue sky. It can take us a while to creep out from our winter hibernation, and the reality doesn't always match the promise. Any of you who have ever taken your family off to enjoy the sunshine and forgotten that, actually, it's still pretty cold, and you should have brought your coats after all, will know this all too well! But we get a fantastic sense of the tipping of the seasons if we brave the outdoors before the shops tell us it's picnic season. We can creep up on spring and listen to its secrets as it bursts into life around us.

Lent is also a season where, as people of faith, we walk quite differently from the mainstream secular world. There is some folk memory of 'giving things up for Lent' but little understanding of the significance and reason for this. This gulf only becomes more obvious as things step up towards Easter, and we find ourselves step-by-step following through the Passion as others relax on a long Easter break. Lent can feel a bit of a marathon as the days stretch into weeks, and the weeks stretch into months, and the joy and new life of Easter feels almost unattainable.

In my experience, though, people are intrigued by what I'm up to. They are attracted to the idea of taking time to think more deeply about things and notice things more. Many people find that they experience spiritual connection more readily when outdoors, and indeed the Bible is full of imagery drawn from the natural world. Creation is well able to speak to us of the creator, and we can take each encounter as our own personal parable, listening to what God wishes to share with us through it. The activities in this book are intended to support you to get out and enjoy creation, to shape your journey as you travel through Lent, and to offer you some chances to share God's creation with others.

HOW TO USE THIS BOOK

Unless there's some crazy weather fluke, it is very unlikely you will start this book at the beginning and work your way through to the end. The book is set out thematically, so I've clumped together a bunch of ideas that are good for a sunny day, for example. So, when you have a better idea of the forecast for the week ahead (for those who like to plan) or when you wake up in the morning and look out of the window (for those who are more spontaneous), you can take your pick of an appropriate activity.

Some of the activities need you to find other people to do them with, or involve a bit more forward planning. Some can be done just as you are, in your socks, with your hair a bit frizzy. The ideas are there to provide you with a pick and mix to create your own wild Lent, and include short reflections to help you listen to what God might be sharing with you through the world he created. You don't have to do an activity every day through the season, although there is enough in here for you to do so if you want, and there's certainly no guilt needed if you miss a day.

In this book, the six weeks of Lent will be loosely structured around the idea of a journey, reflecting both the experience of the Hebrew people in the desert, and Jesus in the wilderness. Hopefully this will make sure that your wild Lent experience isn't simply about doing a bunch of different activities, but gives you a sense of progression towards Easter. Each week of Lent has been given a journeying theme – putting down, picking up, setting off, journeying on, into the wilderness, and finding home.

Each activity will have reflections suitable for a couple of different weeks. It may be that you choose to do the same activity more than once, thinking about it from your different stages of your Lent journey. Don't feel you have to be limited by the focus of my reflections, either. God may be using his creation to prompt you into understanding something completely different from anything I've written, and that's more than fine by me. The thematic index at the back of the book flags up which activities have suitable reflections for each week, at a glance. There's space throughout the book for you to journal about your experience and about what God has given you from it. Hopefully this will become something special to look back on. If you use social media, post your thoughts and pictures under #wildlent, and perhaps you will be inspired by what you see others posting.

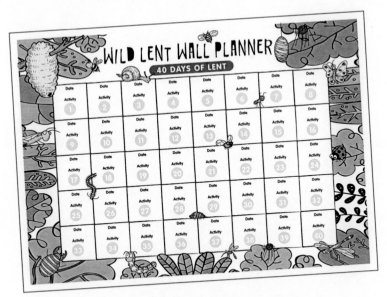

Download the full-colour Wild Lent Wall Planner
to organise your activities for Lent.
Go to **www.kevinmayhew.com/wild-lent.html** and click on resources

THINGS TO DO WHEN IT'S SUNNY

On a Sunny Day...

make a
shadow
Clock

See
page
16

feel the sun

on your face

See
page
20

make a
shadow
sculpture

See
page
18

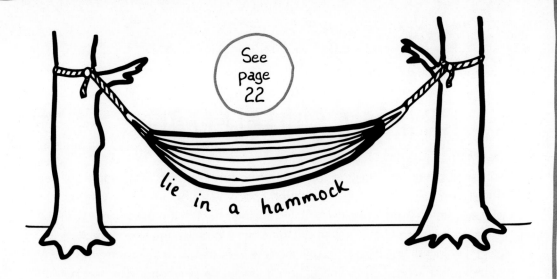

See
page
22

lie in a hammock

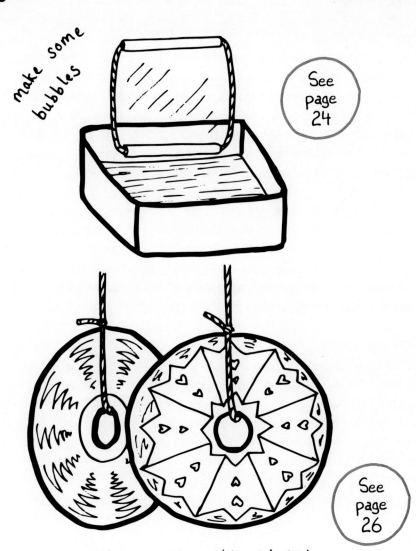

make some bubbles

See
page
24

See
page
26

make rainbows with old CD's

MAKE A SHADOW CLOCK

Sometimes it is very easy to forget that we are living on a spinning ball travelling round a star, hurtling through space. We look out of our window at a still, static world, not a dizzyingly spinning one. But there's an easy way to become aware of our movement, and that's to notice the shadows. As a child, I enjoyed watching how my shadow was as tall as my mum on the school run, became short and squat at lunchtime play, and stretched out again by the evening.

If you have access to some concrete or tarmac space, the simplest form of a shadow clock is to draw a cross on the floor with chalk, and stand on it. Get a friend to draw round your shadow and label it with the time. Every hour, head back out there, stand on the cross, and draw round your shadow again. Note how the length and direction changes as the day goes on, as you've moved relative to the sun. Hopefully it won't rain for a couple of days, and then any time you want to check the time, you can just go and stand on your cross, and see where your shadow falls!

Using slightly more equipment (a stick!) and fewer people (no need for a friend this time!), you could make a shadow clock by poking your stick into a sunny patch of soil or sand outside. Poke in another stick each hour at the edge of the shadow, or mark these with large stones. You could go even more high-tech, and score hour marks on the poked-in sticks, or write the hour in chalk or mud paint on the large stones!

Putting down

As you draw around your shadow, or place a stick or a stone on the ground to mark the movement of the shadow of a stick, you are capturing and preserving how things are at one precise moment. To do this, you have to pay attention and look carefully. At the start of our Lenten journey, it is important for us to stop and see how and where we are, now; to trace our shape and our edges, just as the chalk drew around the details of our shadows. It's important to place a marker on the ground; this is me, as I am. Time moves on. Things change. But sometimes placing a marker is a good point to start from.

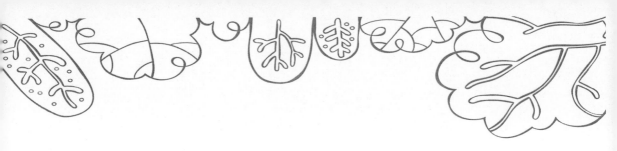

Lord, you know me inside and out. You know my gifts and my failings, my talents and my struggles. Help me to look at myself with love and affection; to see who and where I am, right now. I mark this place with prayerful intention to journey with you this Lent.
Amen.

Journeying on

This type of clock has been around for thousands of years, helping people measure and keep track of time, that invisible force shaping our days. You can't rush time. You can't force the shadow to move, and you can't slow it down. Becoming aware of the movement of the shadow and the movement of our planet can help us to see our journey through life with new eyes. There's a sense of unhurried pace, and a feeling of sway and movement, of repetition and satisfying pattern, and maybe we can begin to be aware of and value this in our own life journey.

Lord, you hold the span of my life within your endless 'now'. I give thanks for your loving care over the years, and look ahead with confidence to your loving care in the future.
Amen.

MAKE A SHADOW SCULPTURE

It's always fun to make ephemeral art outside, knowing that what you're making is beautiful and precious for now, and that you may be the only person to ever enjoy it. This time, have a go at making a piece of art, not for the actual creation itself, but for the effect it has and the shadow it throws.

Collect some sticks and leaves, stones and grasses, and maybe some mud or string to hold it all together. Create something to stand in the sun, but be mindful more of the shadow that falls from it, rather than the look of the sculpture itself. You may make something abstract, a shape that's pleasing to you. You might try to create a shadow of a tree, or a building, or a cityscape skyline. Or perhaps you'd like to try to make an animal or some kind of figure. This is for your own enjoyment, so don't worry that you're not an amazing artist – just enjoy making something for the sake of it.

As the day goes on, watch and enjoy how your shadow picture shifts and changes with the movement of the sun. Maybe you'll notice things about your sculpture that you hadn't realised were there. Perhaps as it changes with time, it'll remind you of different things.

 Picking up

As you wander around collecting materials to create your shadow sculpture, it may be that you have a clear idea in your head of what it is you'd like to make, and what objects will help you make your idea a reality. Or it may be that you pick up things that interest you, and you think, 'Hmm, this might be useful', with no real idea of what you're going to do with it until your fingers get to work. As we get ready to follow Jesus through the journey of our lives, there are elements of both of these things going on. Some things we can plan for and know we must deliberately make time for and prioritise. Some things feel important to us, although we aren't sure why or how yet. The excitement of the journey is seeing how Jesus draws all of it into a glorious whole.

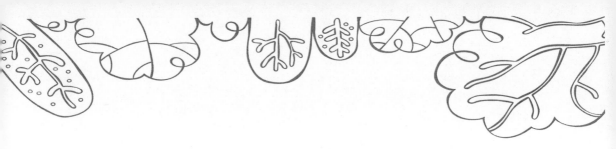

Lord, as I look at my life, I can see the things I do, the relationships I have, my passions and my priorities. Help me to make wise choices, to cherish that which is good and to explore with you how it will shape the person I am becoming.
Amen.

Setting off

It's fine to collect handfuls of sticks, some interesting feathers, long grasses, pebbles, and a variety of leaves but at some point you have to stop collecting and start creating. There's something deeply human about the act of turning one thing into another, of shaping and moulding the environment to our own ends. As we set out on our Christian journey, we do so in a creative spirit, knowing that we will be shaped and changed by God and that through our lives God will be able to shape and change the world.

Lord, thank you that you have created me as a creative being, able to see possibilities and dream ideas. I am excited to see the 'me' you are creating. Help me work with you to create holy change in the world.
Amen.

FEEL THE SUN ON YOUR FACE

There may be sunny days in the winter, but the sun's rays are weak, spread over a larger area. As our half of the earth is tilted away, so we see the sun at a lower angle. As the angle of our planet shifts, and we begin to tilt back towards the sun, the sun's rays intensify, giving them more power over a smaller area, and the sun climbs higher in the sky.

There comes a day in the spring when the sun is out and you feel it warming your face, or soaking through your sleeves. You suddenly remember feeling this before, after the winter has almost erased all memory of a warm sun.

Find a sheltered spot, maybe near a wall (it's not for nothing that stately homes used walled gardens to coax their earliest crops) and stand or sit so that the sun falls full on your face. Close your eyes and see the brightness seeping through your eyelids, filling your mind with a pink glow. Feel the sun's radiation stroking, tickling and nuzzling your eyebrows, your cheeks, your ears. Feel the warmth of the sun, that's travelled so many thousands of miles to get to you, finally soak into your skin.

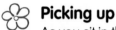 **Picking up**

As you sit in the sun, soaking up the early spring warmth, think also of sitting in the presence of the Almighty. Feel the sun's rays play over your face and feel yourself basking in the love of the God who loves you. As the warmth from the sun wriggles into your shoulders, unknotting and loosening your muscles, know that the warmth of God will strengthen you with love in your life. The power from the sun is liberally poured over you; so also is the power of God, filling you with all good gifts – love, joy, peace, patience, kindness, goodness, faithfulness, gentleness and self-control.

> Lord, thank you for filling me with your warmth, your power and your love. Help me to glow with your light, to warm others with your presence. Amen.

Finding home

The sun is on average about 150 million kilometres away from you, as you sit or stand there in the spring light. The light and the heat have already travelled for eight minutes through space, much further than any human has ever gone. And yet, of all the many places out there in the solar system, or on our own planet, where these photons could have landed, they have landed on you. At the end of all our journeying, we sometimes find ourselves, and realise the chance of us even existing is so small, and yet here we are, precious and loved by God.

Lord, thank you for reminding me that I am precious and special. Thank you for all I have learned about myself this Lent, and for the person I am constantly on a journey to discover. Amen.

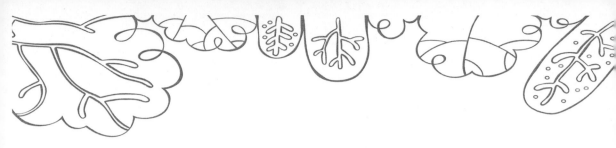

LIE IN A HAMMOCK

I first bought a hammock when I was 8. I'd lie in my backyard watching the spiders crawl into their holes in the brickwork, and be still for literally minutes at a time. This was no mean feat for the 8-year-old me. I still find a hammock allows me to be calm in a way I find difficult to access otherwise. There's something about the gentle movement and enfolding fabric that settles and stills me.

I have a large South American hammock in my garden, and there are times I know I need to give myself some hammock time. Just a few minutes will do. I have a smaller hammock in parachute nylon for forest school sessions, that I picked up online for just over a tenner. It gets an awful lot of use over the sessions I teach in a week, with staff often surprised at how certain children unexpectedly gravitate to the hammock, often the children they expect to spend the session haring around busily rather than just chilling out.

So grab your hammock and head out to find two suitable trees. If you've got a cheap hammock, you may need to choose your trees wisely, so that the hammock hangs happily between them, just the right distance apart. Tie your knots securely. A simple reef knot will suffice; that's right over left, left over right, and should look flat if you've tied it right. If it looks twisted you've tied a granny knot. Tie it again, and pay more attention to your rights and your lefts this time!

A hammock forces you to change your perspective. Instead of looking ahead, you're now looking up, right into the tree canopy and beyond that to the skies. You're aware of the movement all around you, as each tree and branch sways, and you sway with them. You're aware of the birds, some darting from tree to tree, some setting up stage on a branch above you to give you your own private concert, some flying strong and high, off on a journey. You feel supported and yet you know how ephemeral, how temporary your resting place is.

✿ Setting off

There's a real sense of movement about setting off on a journey. After all the preparation, you're off. Your legs are still untired. You haven't yet faced any of the trials or seen any of the wonders of the journey, but you have set your face to a new direction. You are looking away from your starting point towards where you will travel. A hammock gives you that sense of movement, that sense of facing a new direction, without you even going anywhere! As you lie in your hammock, enjoy your perspective-shift, and ponder which direction you are going to face to continue your Lenten journey.

> Lord, I am ready to travel with you.
> Keep my feet moving along your path,
> and my face turned towards your love.
> Amen.

✿ Finding home

We think of home as solidity, as permanence. We can see the pain and heartbreak of those who have had to leave their home because of famine, war, or climate change, every day on the news. You may have created a new home yourself, in a new place, among new people, and know the challenges you've faced to do so. A hammock is certainly not solidity or permanence. And yet it speaks of home. We are all strangers and pilgrims, journeying through the world and through our lives. This is not our final destination – we are seeking the city of God. We should not wish to erect a permanent solid edifice around our faith, but must always keep moving, slinging our hammock between the trees, and being aware of the movement of God all around us, and within us. Our home is within the dance of the Trinity, in the very movement within the heart of God himself.

> Lord, as I find my home within you,
> keep me conscious of the movement of
> your Spirit around me and within me.
> Amen.

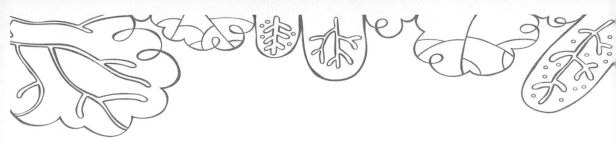

BLOW BUBBLES

Don't you think bubbles look just beautiful floating off into a blue sky? My kids would tell you I have a bit of a thing about bubbles. I blame it on my mother. She didn't want to buy me sweets in case they rotted my teeth, so bought me tube after tube of bubble mix. I spent happy hours trotting round the garden blowing bubbles. It's so addictive – you blow one bubble, and are convinced you'll be able to blow an even better one next time . . . next time . . . next time! When I make bubble mix for us to play with in the garden, my kids virtually have to wrestle the bubble wand out of my fingers.

The secret to making good bubble mixture is to use branded un-eco-friendly washing-up liquid. They add stuff to make that extra bubbly so you think it's working better – not so great going down the sink into the water system, but it's what you want for good bubbles. Very gently mix one cup of this with nine cups of water. Try not to make it bubbly – to blow good bubbles you need the bubble mix bubble-free. If you have glycerin in the house (or can buy some) add one tablespoon – this will stop the bubbles popping so fast and give you a more satisfying time.

Next, you need some wool or string, and a drinking straw. Cut the straw in half and thread the wool or string through both halves, one after another, until you can make a kind of square/circle thing. Tie the wool ends together, and pick it up by one of the straws – the bottom straw should hang down, pulling the wool into a square/circle shape. Dip all of this in a bowl of bubble mix. Lift it back out and check you have a 'window'– see-through bubble mix coating the space between the straws and the wool. Waft around your garden, and you should easily be able to make large bubbles appear.

If you are getting twitchy at the thought of plastic straws (sorry! I am trying to cut my plastic use too!), you can cut two lengths of elder, and poke out the spongey bit with a metal tent peg. I used these wands with a bunch of 2- to 3-year-olds, and they managed pretty well and loved making the bubbles.

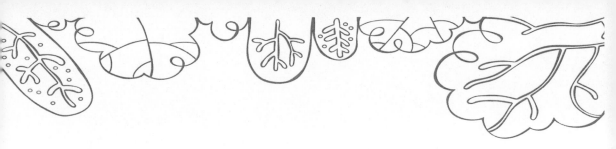

Setting off

As you pause, with a window of bubble mixture on your wand, and feel the breeze about to waft it into a bubble, you can already see in your mind's eye the bubble you hope it will become. It's good to get the balance right between living in the present moment, attuned to the wind and the shimmer of the mixture, and having hope for the future, imagining the bubble sailing away above the roof. So also for us this Lent – we live in the moment of 40 days and nights of prayer and fasting, whilst looking forward with hope to the resurrection.

> Lord, I can see clearly where I am. This ground, this sky, this weather, this moment. Help me to see as clearly the signs of your eternal kingdom. Amen.

Into the wilderness

Blowing good bubbles is an exercise in keeping on keeping on. Practising something doesn't come naturally to me – I get bored quite easily – but there's such an instant gratification with bubble blowing that I'll happily keep at it for ages and struggle to relinquish the bubble wand to someone else. Sometimes you dip the bubble wand and your window pops instantly. Sometimes you almost make the perfect bubble but then it bursts just before completion. With each missed bubble, you get a better sense of how to blow your best yet, and it's surely just around the corner. As we walk our faith, we sometimes stumble, we sometimes mess up and we sometimes wander off and get a bit lost. But these missteps can help us gain a better sense of how our faith should look when at its best and most God-reflecting.

> Lord, sometimes I find that faith can be a struggle. Sometimes my prayer life feels dry or, as soon as I get into a pattern of reading the Scriptures, I lose my rhythm once again. Help me to use even these difficulties to shape my faith and make it clearer to me. Amen.

MAKE A RAINBOW

There are plenty of ways for you to make a rainbow, as long as you have a sunny day. Keep the sun behind you and turn on the hose. Squish your thumb over the edge so the water sprays out (you might need to get prepared with waterproof coat and trousers!) and if the mist is fine enough, you should see rainbows in the spray.

Alternatively, dig around in your old CD/DVD collection for any you don't play any more. Catch the sun with the disc and throw out a rainbow onto a wall or a sheet. If you think it would be fun to make a fancier rainbow, you can cut out a circle the same size as the disc, fold and cut as you would if you were making a Christmas snowflake, and tape it on to the disc. Try several patterns and enjoy how the rainbow changes.

Of course, if you have any chunky glass prisms from an old light fitting (the faux chandelier type of thing), you can do a 'Pollyanna', and hang it in such a way that the light travels through and makes rainbows dance on the wall opposite.

Journeying on

A rainbow is a very beautiful optical illusion, but an illusion all the same. Nobody sees quite the same rainbow – it's all to do with the angle of the light that bounces out of the raindrops towards our eyes. The white light we see is made up of light of different wavelengths. When the light passes through a different material (the water, or a prism, or the coating of a CD) the different wavelengths pass through at different speeds, so they end up leaving the material at slightly different times. This splits the light up into its component colours visible to our eyes. Interestingly, the colours of a rainbow are a phenomenon peculiar to the human eye. A black and white photograph simply shows a bow of increasing and decreasing brightness. A moonbow, although essentially the same thing seen by the light of a bright moon, is perceived as white, simply because our eyes are not good at seeing colours in dim light.

We all travel towards God at different speeds. Our journey of faith doesn't necessarily follow the same path that anyone else has travelled. But that

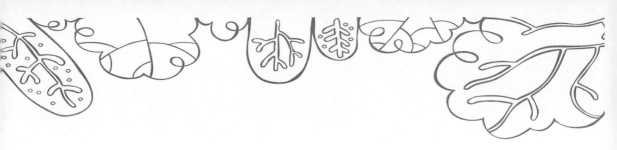

isn't something to concern or worry us. It is in our beautiful diversity that we arrive in the heavenly kingdom, as the rainbow people of God.

> Lord, help me to remember that I travel on my own journey with you and to you; a journey that is mine, and spectacularly suited to me in a way that no other journey could be.
> Amen.

Into the wilderness

Thinking of rainbows leads me first to remember the story of Noah, lost in the wilderness of the devastating flood, and of the joy at dry land and God's promise. It reminds me of the struggle for equality and acceptance of the LGBT community, and of pride in place of shame. It calls to mind Desmond Tutu's phrase, 'The rainbow people of God' which depicts a joyful celebration after the horrors of apartheid. There's a coming-together in a rainbow, a celebration of difference, and the light waves we see form something beautiful, coming together again after they have travelled a different journey. As we inhabit our own wilderness, we look with hope to the rainbow ahead – a rainbow of joy, promise, pride and celebration.

> Lord, as the bleakness of my own wilderness surrounds me, remind me of the stories of others who have emerged from the wilderness to a place of peace and joy, and help me to look ahead with hope to the rainbow I know will come.
> Amen.

NOTES

There are extra pages for your own notes at the end of the book.

THINGS TO DO WHEN IT'S RAINING

On a Rainy Day . . .

put up a tarp
and shelter beneath it

See
page
32

START

FINISH

See
page
36

Race some snails

let the rain
paint a picture

See
page
38

See
page
40

catch some raindrops
on a leaf

See
page
42

make a mud face in a tree

make a raindrop orchestra

See
page
44

PUT UP A TARP AND SHELTER BENEATH IT

One of the most satisfying things I learned to do on my forest school practitioners training course, was to put up a shelter using only a rope and a square of tarp. After countless den-building expeditions to the woods, it was so exciting for me to be able to quickly knock up a shelter that actually worked in reality rather than just my imagination!

First, you need to source yourself a rope (or some paracord) and a tarp. Nearly everyone has at least one tarp hanging around, stuffed in a cupboard or in the garage and covered in spiders, or thrown over some garden chairs and populated by snails. If you don't, they're cheap to pick up, and I'm sure you'll find a use for yours afterwards (and so will the spiders and snails). Ropes seem to turn up in cheap supermarkets and pound shops, in DIY shops and garden centres, or in the local military hardware store.

Take your rope and tarp for a walk into woodland. Find two trees that are a comfortable distance away from each other, without too many spikey prickles beneath (or you'll have a most uncomfortable dry spot!). Tie one end of the rope around one of the trees, using a tension hitch. This is where you wind the rope once around the tree, and then snake it back on itself, tucking it and threading it round and round the rope around the tree. This should be enough to hold it firm, as long as tension is applied. Walk the long end of your rope across to the other tree. You need to make sure you tie a knot that will keep the tension in the rope to support the weight of the tarp (and any rain that's falling!).

I suggest a triangular tension knot – wrap the rope around the trunk once, flop it over the rope line you've made, and pull it back around the trunk the other way. Once you've met the rope you started with, the ropes will draw a triangle. Tuck the end into the triangle and pull. Finish off with a couple of half hitches, or something similar, to keep it all in place.

Fling your tarp over the top, and either peg down the corners or find some suitable sticks to poke through the eyelets and into the ground. Depending

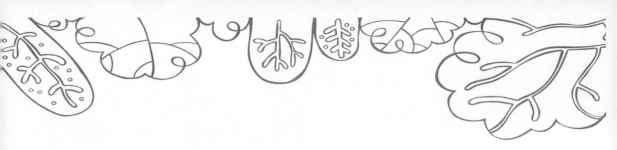

on how high your line is, you may need to tie on some string to attach the tarp to the pegs in the ground. Climb inside out of the rain, and listen to the sound of the raindrops on the shelter. Feel cosy and safe. Maybe pull out a flask of tea or hot chocolate, and have a biscuit or two. If the water is really cascading off the edges, younger members of your party may like to see how much they can catch in their cup, when they've finished their drink.

Picking up

Before an expedition, it's important to source the right kit. If you were setting off into the woodland to make a shelter on a dry sunny day, you might only need to pack a sheet to act as a pretend tent, with some string to hang it, but this rainy expedition is different. Your very comfort and health depend on you kitting up correctly. You need the real deal – genuine waterproof tarp and strong durable rope or paracord. As we journey through Lent, and through our lives, we need to make sure we are expedition-ready and that what we collect to support us is the real deal. We need the strong, durable law of love, rather than the law of niceties or culturally acceptable behaviour.

> Lord, as I travel through this Lent and through my life, help me to kit myself out with your love. Your love to support me and your love through me to support others. Amen.

Into the wilderness

Your local forest or woodland may not feel very much like wilderness. I know the patch of woodland I often use is sandwiched between the council dump, allotments, a playpark, and plenty of residential housing. It's used by all manner of people for all manner of activities, legal and illegal! But it is still wild and untamed, the brambles bursting from the ground ready to ensnare the ill-placed foot. I have no control over it.

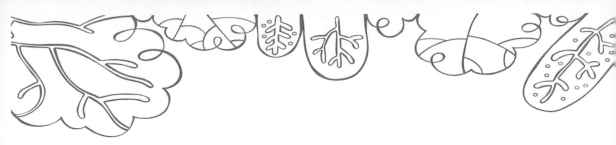

It isn't always an easy or a safe place. And yet, it is still somewhere full of beauty, where I can find peace. And when it's raining, a place where I can create shelter, albeit temporary. Our place of shelter and safety as Christians is within the love of God, which travels with us even to the wildest places.

Lord, in your love I find shelter and safety.
As I live through storms, help me to feel your
love surrounding me and protecting me.
Amen.

WILD
LENT

HOLD A SNAIL RACE

Some of my best friends when I was a young child were snails. I'd collect them in the garden and take them for rides on my tricycle, as I felt they'd enjoy a bit of a burst of speed being such slow creatures. On a rainy day, you can collect a good jug or ice-cream tub-full quickly, searching round the flowerbeds for slithering treasure.

Snails are pretty impossible to train – you can't persuade them to race in a straight line – so unless you find particularly intelligent snails, set your race up by drawing a circle, with a small start-line circle right in the middle. Put your snails inside the middle circle, and give them a countdown. Ok, you don't have to do a countdown, as the snails can't count, but it adds to the drama.

Pull your hood up and settle down to watch the race. Sometimes you'll get a snail who does nothing but blow bubbles, or a snail who tries to catch a piggy back some of the way. Sometimes your front-runner will lose interest and the bubble blower will suddenly wake up and sprint to the finish.

 Putting down

I expect your snails were busy doing something else when you went and collected them from round your garden. They were probably munching those first green shoots of whatever you were hoping to grow in your garden this spring. But if you're slithering over a leaf, scraping off bits of it with your teeth on your foot, you can't do a race at the same time. Maybe at this point, at the beginning of Lent, we need to have a think about what it is we are busying ourselves with, and whether it's something we need to put down for a while to concentrate on the race in hand.

> Lord, sometimes when I am so deep in busyness,
> it is hard to see what I am busying myself with
> and what I'm missing out on. Give me sight to
> see clearly and to make good judgements.
> Amen.

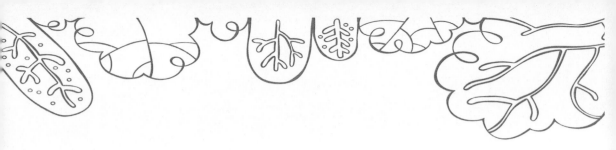

Into the wilderness

I've found that the younger you are, the more frustrating you find it when 'your' snail decides to slither off in totally the wrong direction, or gets sidetracked by a small patch of algae on the concrete. If something is set up as a race, we start thinking in terms of speed and which is 'best'. But being older these days, I'm quite happy to support the snail who isn't winning. To enjoy watching it glisten as it moves along; to see the ripples in its body and the swirls on its shell; to notice the breathing hole damply open and close in its side. One day I may even be able to support myself when I'm not 'winning'– to simply accept and enjoy my 'me'-ness, as I know God does, regardless of my speed or whether I'm best at this or that.

Lord, as I sit, watch and enjoy those snails, all of them, the winners and the losers, the racers and the bubble blowers, I become aware that you watch and enjoy all of us, just as we are. Amen.

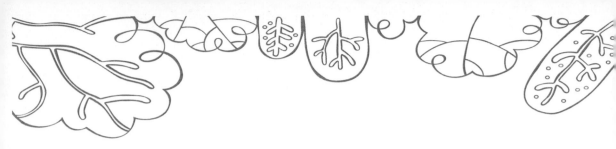

LET THE RAIN PAINT A PICTURE

You don't have to be particularly artistic for this, don't worry. Hopefully you've got a set of watercolour paints squirrelled away in some cupboard or another – this is the day to use them. Take a piece of paper – a sheet of A4 printer paper is fine – and cover it in wet paint splodges and swirls. Keep the paint as wet as you can.

As soon as you're done, dash out into the rain. Put your paper down somewhere not too soggy – not right in the middle of a puddle – and weight it down with a stone on each corner so it doesn't blow away.

The rain will do the rest. As the water drops fall on the paint, they will create patterns and begin to mix some of the different colours into each other. When you're happy with your joint art effort, you and the rain, take it back inside to dry. If it's still pouring, you could maybe make another one! No two will ever be quite the same.

Setting off

The corridor leading to my garden door is full of seven large washing baskets. My mad dash to get a painty piece of paper outside before the rain stops is less of a sprint than a crazy laundry-filled obstacle course. No matter how chaotic or otherwise your house is, you're going to have to move fast after preparing your paper, before the paint dries on it completely and your chance to make collaborative art with the rain dries out too. Once our spiritual preparation is done, we need to have this same eagerness to move on in our journey this Lent. Just as we'll never create rain art if we always stay in the kitchen perfecting our paintwork, our faith will only grow if we follow through on the promises and challenges we have spent time thinking and praying about. Dash out and start collecting those raindrops.

Lord, thank you for giving me your wisdom, for exciting me about growing my faith. Give me an urgency to start to live in your kingdom life today. Amen.

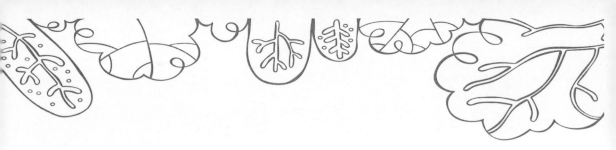

✿ Finding home

I wonder how much your idea of when your rain art was finished was brought about by the rain starting to trickle in through your collar, or through those creases in your coat sleeve. (Why do waterproofs lose their waterproofing so irritatingly soon after buying a new coat?) Were you able to stand and watch the drops splashing and the picture they were creating, without being distracted by the drip forming at the end of your nose? What does 'finished' look like anyway? Certainly, if you'd left the picture for too much longer it would have turned into rather muddy papier mâché. It's about feeling happy with how it is and about seizing that moment. If eternity is the moment we are seizing, how do we know where it is? Hopefully some of your wild experiences this Lent have given you a glimpse into the beauty and wonder of God's eternal kingdom. Now all we have to do is keep on training ourselves to see it every day.

Lord, it has been so good to catch glimpses of your eternal kingdom of beauty, peace and love. Help my eyes stay open to you, so that the more I see, the more I know myself to have found my true home in you.
Amen.

REFLECTIONS IN RAINDROPS

This is one for after the rain has eased a bit, unless you've got a really waterproof camera! One of the brilliant things about the rise of the smartphone is that almost everyone has access to a camera. Sometimes it is good to live life lens-free; I'm as guilty as the next person is for constantly looking at my life to see how it'll fit in a photo. But looking through a camera can also become a useful discipline to help you really see what you're looking at. It enables you to notice the details, to see how one part fits in with another and have an idea of perspective, shape, composition, distance and colour.

As the rain stops, take your camera out to try to capture some of that just-washed detail of the day. Although I have a 'proper' camera, I do usually end up using my smartphone. As photographer friends of mine quote, the best camera is the one you have with you. This is about capturing the moment.

See if you can find some raindrops on a leaf. Notice the bulge of them. See how they glisten and bring out the details of the leaf beneath. If the light is right, can you see the world around you caught within the surface tension of the water? Can you find any puddles, reflecting the storm-swept sky above you? Or the swirly rainbows of oil, if you live near a road.

 Picking up

A collection of photos is an interesting thing. It doesn't take up very much space at all, especially if you don't print them out! It's one of the only collections where what you're collecting is left undisturbed after you've left (memories being another!). What it does take from you is a readiness to look at things closely, and to make decisions about what you want your photo to look like. Here, you are collecting moments in time, choosing yourself what is beautiful, what is interesting, and what is surprising. Let us also look at our lives closely, to see where the surprising beauty is and to bring it with us, to notice the reflections of God's grace and love.

Lord, help me to look closely at each of my moments to see the beauty within and the reflections of your love in my life. Amen.

Journeying on

A surprising thing happens when you start noticing. You have probably walked through this outside space or a similar one, after rain, many times before. If you were focusing on where you were heading, on staying dry, or thinking about what to cook for dinner, you probably didn't notice the sparkling drops around you. And once you do, you start to see more. You see the reflections of the sky above and the magnifying effect of the raindrop on the leaf. You see the swirls in the puddles and the colours of the stones when they're wet. As we continue on our journey of faith, we need to slow down and notice the beauty of God around us as we go, as well as looking ahead to the glory that is to come.

Lord, thank you that all of life is touched with your glory. Help me to notice your beauty around me as I go, and for that to give me strength for the journey. Amen.

MUD FACES

I'm lucky in that the soil where I live is comprised mostly of London clay. It makes digging the garden a whole body workout and if it rains, my garden turns into a lake, but if I'm wanting good mud to work with, I've come up trumps.

Rainy days are perfect for mixing up some good mud to play with. Go for the stickiest mix you can for this – dig some mud and mix with extra water if it's not raining quite hard enough. Mix the mud until you can squidge it into a ball without it crumbling into pieces. For this activity, you need a tree, or two or three, so take your mud on a tree-finding trip if there aren't any nearby. You're looking for trees with character, with knobbly, bobbly bits.

Take a good look at your trees. See if you can try to catch a glimpse of their character, or the character they would have if they were people, not trees. Where's their nose? Where would their eyes go? Are they old or young? Cheeky or grumpy? Wise or foolish? Get your mud and start making your trees come alive, pushing mud eyes onto the bark, embellishing the nose and picking out the details of the lips. You could add old seeds, twigs and grasses that you find on the ground. Maybe your tree face needs hair, or a twiggy crown. If you're doing this activity with others, split up to make your own tree face, and then introduce your personality to the rest of the group.

 **Picking up**

I don't know when you last played with mud. I'm guessing it might have been as a child, when you mixed mud pies. Maybe more recently, you have crafted with clay, although that's a more sterile experience, without bits of stick and grass stuck inside! There's a natural squeamishness towards mud. We don't like getting ourselves mucky. We don't always like the idea of damp and dirt on our hands. We think about germs and microbes, and about how long it will be until we can get to a nice hot tap and some soap. I've had to train myself to enjoy mud as part of my job. Often adults (and some children too) can't quite bring themselves to actually pick up a handful of mud, but are keen to do the muddy activity. Surprisingly, I often find that they're happy

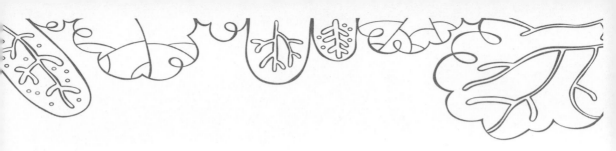

for me to pick the mud up for them and place it in their hands, and that once that initial aversion has passed, the sensory experience of mud play is actually enjoyable. Sometimes we find that we have an initial aversion to the discipline of formal daily prayer, or Bible reading, or maybe building a relationship with someone we find difficult. It is often surprising how much we value these things once we've schooled ourselves to do them.

> Lord, give me the strength and the courage
> to grasp the disciplines you call me to, in the
> knowledge that what I hold I will come to cherish.
> Amen.

Finding home

Spending time with a tree gives you a real sense of connection with the rest of the created world. You are both living and growing organisms, that have changed through time partly because of your DNA and partly as a result of the environment you've lived in. And, just as you were able to see beyond the bark and the leaves to the tree within, so also we trust that God sees beyond any front that we present to the person we truly are. We have nothing to fear from this seeing; what God has created is loved and precious to him. Our lives are held safe within his loving care.

> Lord, thank you that you can see the 'me' you
> created, and that you love and cherish me as
> I am. Help me also to see the person I truly am,
> and as precious and loved.
> Amen.

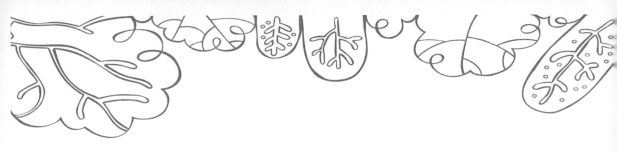

RAINDROP ORCHESTRA

One of my favourite sounds is rain on a tent canvas. There's something quite exhilarating about the rhythm of the raindrops and the tune they sing as you lie there (hopefully) staying dry and cosy inside.

Have a go at getting the raindrops to play you a rainy day symphony by giving them some different things to splash and drip onto. A length of silver foil, weighted down with rocks on the corners to stop it blowing away, should give you high-pitched, pitter-patter sounds. A large metal bowl will give you more reverberating bongs, changing in tone as the bowl fills with water. A biscuit tin will give you louder clangs, or bongs if it's a plastic one. Have a raid on your kitchen and bathroom to see what you can find to experiment with.

Put your raincoat on, put up your umbrella and set up the players in your orchestra. Experiment with putting them out in the open, or under somewhere drippy like an overhanging branch or a leaf-blocked gutter. Enjoy how the sound changes with the rain, soft and reflective while the rain is gentle; deafening and boisterous as the rain pelts down in sheets. Maybe it seems to you that the rain is speaking to you, giving you a message; maybe the rhythm of the rain is calling words to mind. Maybe you can add some words to the rhythm on purpose – verses of Scripture, half-remembered prayers.

Putting down

It's hard to predict what kind of sound your objects will make in the rain before you put them down in it. You can imagine what they might do, and I expect you did this as you walked round your house collecting things. But you don't actually know until you put them out under the raindrops. Sometimes objects you think will have a great effect end up doing very little, and that extra something you picked up just in case is actually brilliant. So too our habits and beliefs, the things we hold dear. As we test out each of these at the beginning of Lent, we find which are life-giving, and which may look and sound good but don't work as we need them to.

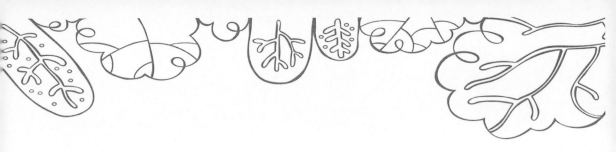

Lord, I offer you my habits and my beliefs,
those things I cling to and believe are important.
Give me clarity to listen to which of these
resound with your life and your love, and
strength to put down those that don't.
Amen.

Journeying on

As we continue on our spiritual journey, the sights and sounds we encounter on our way sometimes call to mind our destination and our resolve to journey there. Sometimes it is in the places and people we would expect – a beautiful church building, an uplifting hymn or song of praise, an inspiring person of faith. But sometimes it's the places and people outside of this who feed and inspire our faith as we travel. It might be through kindness shown us at the market stall or the hospital car park; the flowering weeds outside the supermarket at the edge of the road; the joy the feral pigeons have in their flight. The more we are able to notice the beauty around us, the glimpses of God's kingdom, the more we will be able to hear the reverberations and echoes of the kingdom we are travelling to. Just as the raindrops beat out a message of peace and freedom, exhilaration and awe, so also does the world around us.

Lord, as I hear the song of the raindrops,
your creation giving you praise, give me ears
to hear the song of all creation, and for that
to encourage me on my journey to heaven.
Amen.

NOTES

There are extra pages for your own notes at the end of the book.

THINGS TO DO WITH OTHERS

Things to do with others...

See page 50

go on a sunrise breakfast walk

See page 54

build a giant nest and
sit in it

See page 56

enjoy an Easter egg hunt

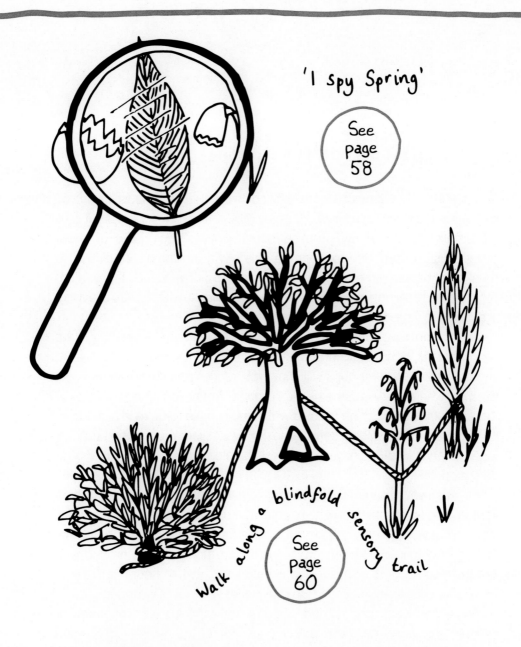

'I spy Spring'

See
page
58

Walk along a blindfold sensory trail

See
page
60

hide in the
bushes and
play Eagle Eye

See
page
62

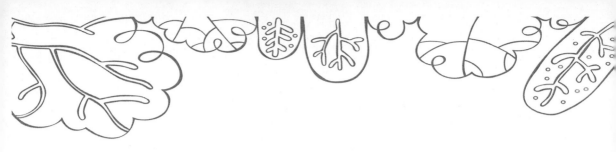

SUNRISE BREAKFAST WALK

This is quite a good time of year to try to catch the sunrise. At least it won't be as early in the morning as it would be by May or June! Nevertheless, it is all too tempting to roll over and promise yourself that you'll go another day. Your duvet is just so warm and comfortable. This is why making a commitment to meet other people is a good idea. If you know you have friends that you are meant to be meeting, who are relying on you to get out of bed, you are more likely to keep your date with the dawn.

Check what time sunrise is where you are. It'll vary as to how early in the year Lent falls, or how far north or south in the country you are. It's easy to find out – most weather apps will show you sunrise and sunset times. Next, work out where there is some high(er) ground, where you have a good view facing east. It's going to be tricky to watch the sunrise if you're in a valley, or if you have a large building complex to the east of you. Your phone probably has a compass feature, or you can check the place you're thinking of visiting on a map.

It's nice if you can meet up and walk together through the pale morning light, ending up at your spot of high ground just a few minutes before sunrise. It doesn't have to be a long walk, but it's pleasant to walk together and enjoy the night lightening, being aware of the expectancy of the life around you. Are there some trees or bushes you could walk past, to hear the rustlings within them? It's likely to be cold, so make sure you're well wrapped up.

Arrive at your high ground and face east. You can see the sky brightening, even if it's going to be a dull day. Then suddenly the glimmer of the sun emerges over the horizon, brighter and stronger than you could have imagined just a few moments ago. If you don't mind looking daft, get down and push the planet round towards the sun. If not, feel your feet stuck with gravity to the ground, as your spaceship earth rolls forwards. You can almost feel the world moving and you tipping! Rather than the sun coming to you, you can begin to sense Earth moving round so that the bit you are standing on is coming round into the light.

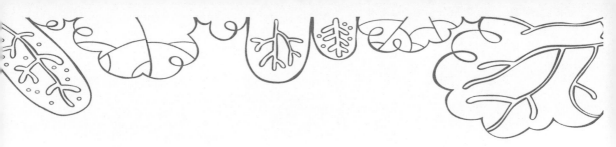

Make sure you've brought some breakfast with you. You may not feel hungry when you stumble, sleep-drunk, from your front door, but it's amazing how watching the dawn gives you an appetite. A flask of hot coffee, tea, or hot chocolate will feel very welcome. Muesli bars are easy, honey or jam sandwiches are traditional, but sausages, hot from the frying pan, wrapped up in foil and a few layers of tea towels, stuffed in a cool bag, and eaten in rolls with ketchup or brown sauce, will make you feel you're breakfasting like a king.

Setting off

The sunrise symbolises a new start like nothing else. It's unmissable. Staring out east towards the horizon, there's no chance that you won't notice that glowing, almost vibrating, ball of fire appear. The new day has definitely started. Here we are too, setting off on our journey of faith, tipping towards the journey that is ahead of us. As we look forward to what is ahead, we are also aware of how things are changing all around us. As the dawn breaks, the colours brighten, and the life around us wakes up and moves; so also we notice how, as we set off to follow Jesus, the world changes around us. We notice God's love and peace, and the ripples from us following him faithfully spread out across the world.

> Lord, as my journey tips me towards you,
> I give thanks for the beauty around me that
> your love brings into focus. May my life reflect
> your love and light to others.
> Amen.

Finding home

If we notice the sun, it is normally from our perspective. We enjoy the light coming through the trees, we bask in the light from a rainbow, we squint into the sun as we drive due west in the winter. Watching the sunrise reminds us of what we know but seldom notice; that the sun is not 'up there' for our benefit or annoyance, but is a massive ball of fire for which our whole

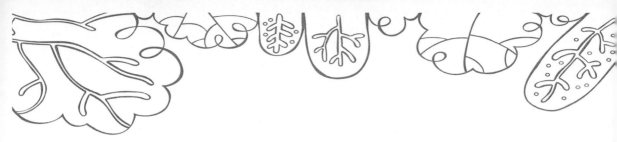

solar system turns. That sense of standing on the edge of a spinning ball, falling forwards almost into the sun as our planet turns, while it continues on its yearly journey orbiting our star, shifts our perspective. We get a better sense of this planet as our home, and of our home's place in the universe. As this Lent draws to a close, we have found our perspective altered. The God whom we have been seeking has all the time been holding us and loving us, from even before we began our journey. And God's kingdom is vaster, and more surprising, than we could ever have imagined.

Lord, thank you that I am able to live on the skin of this planet, which dances its path round its star. Help me to keep this sense of perspective in my dealings with the world, and remind me often of the surprising nature of your love.
Amen.

WILD
LENT

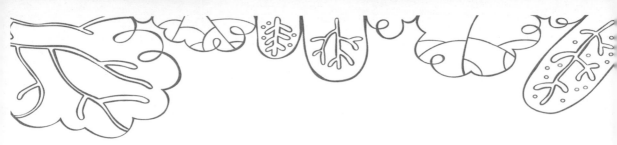

GIANT NEST BUILDING

We were set the task of building a giant nest as a group on my forest school practitioner's training course. We were also asked to compose a song in the style of a musical to introduce our nest to the other groups but I won't ask you to do this bit! We had to build a nest we could all get inside, and we ended up weak-legged from laughing (that might have been the bad singing – if you feel things are getting too serious then maybe do try a musical number after all!).

You'll probably need to travel a little for this. You are looking for a fairly heavily wooded area, where there'll be enough trees for large boughs and branches to have fallen down. Keep an eye on the weather forecast – as you'll be working under trees, you need to make sure that the wind isn't too strong. Look particularly at the strength of the gusts – anything over 30mph may compromise that creaky bough just above you, with dire consequences.

Decide what shape and size your nest needs to be, then start dragging over branches to lay down and start creating. How tall will you make the sides of your nest? How will you keep the branches together? Will your nest be neat like a blackbird's, woven like a reed warbler's, cosy like a wren's, or scruffy like a pigeon's? Will you line it with something to make it warm and snuggly inside?

Once your nest is completed, help each other to climb in. You may feel like doing a little cheeping! Enjoy the feeling of safety and warmth that being cuddled up with your fellow baby birds engenders (and ignore that prickly stick digging into your back). If you've brought a flask of something hot to the woods with you, this might be a good time to bring it out and share it around.

❀ Picking up

As you were walking around the woodland, selecting materials for your nest, you carry with you a sort of 'shape' in your head of what it is you need next. At least, I know I do. I may not know exactly what it is I'm looking for, but I can feel the shape of what I'm after and recognise it

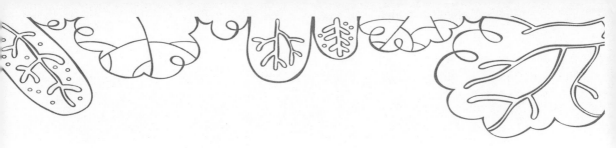

when I see it. You choose your branches with care, knowing which ones will make your nest strong, and you are able to identify some kind of soft lining to make your nest safe and comfortable, even if you weren't sure what you'd have available to use. You place your branches with care, too, making sure you put them where they'll best fit, not just piling them on the ground. This is also true of our habits and practices. This is a good time to mentally walk around our woodland ground, choosing our habits with care, knowing which practices will make our faith strong, and finding what will make our faith safe and somewhere we want to be and to grow in.

> Lord, as I wander around the woodland floor, help me also to choose carefully from among my habits and my practices only those which will help me build a strong faith, and a faith in which I can grow. Amen.

Into the wilderness

Now, unless I'm mistaken, you are not a bird. Nest building may not come naturally to you. Building a nest is something instinctive for birds; they don't have to be taught or shown how to do it. And if you are lucky enough to stumble across an actual bird's nest, even the messiest of crow's nests will make you feel quite inadequate. Is there something that comes so naturally for you that you aren't even aware of how special your skill is? How is your unique nature woven in and around that of others to create something stronger and more beautiful?

> Lord, help me to cherish and value those things which I can do, and can do well. Show me where best to use my talents with others to create something strong and beautiful in your kingdom. Amen.

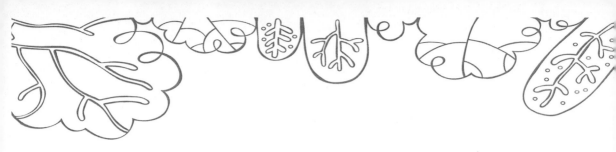

EGG HUNT

Yes, I know it's not Easter yet. Bear with me and don't get offended! As far as the secular calendar goes, chocolate eggs are fair game any time from now. There are plenty of them in the shops; and schools, community groups, and the National Trust (who famously missed out the word 'Easter' recently) offer family Easter egg hunts beginning any time from latish Lent onwards.

Maybe we can get a bit too precious about this. Eggs have been used as a symbol of spring and fertility for many thousands of years, long predating the use of them in the Christian church. If people are happy to hunt for eggs, then maybe we're missing a trick by not engaging with them. Hunting for eggs has got lots of good stuff just waiting to be unpacked – the spirituality around searching being worth a bit of effort when we find hidden treasure. I expect children have been sent off on egg hunts for thousands of years, ever since the first chickens were domesticated and didn't always conveniently flap back to their nest box.

What are you going to provide for the hunt? Bags of small chocolate eggs are sold everywhere and are pretty cheap. I've cut egg shapes out of old Christmas cards before now, and then cut each of those in half using different zig-zag patterns. I then hid one half of each egg, and gave the other half out to the children doing the hunting, for them to find their missing egg half. At my forest school session this Easter holiday, we cut wood cookies (circles about a centimetre or two thick from an old branch) using a bowsaw, then decorated them with sharpie pens before hiding them to be found.

Will you mark out a trail, with arrows made out of sticks showing the way along woodland paths? Or will you have enough eggs (or 'eggs') to scatter them around in the long grass and under bushes, and then collect them all together and share them out at the end? Maybe you fancy writing some clues in (bad) verse to lead from one cache of eggs to another.

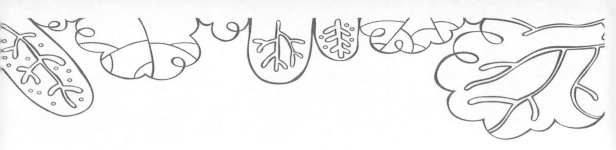

Putting down

It can feel a little incongruous, scattering and hiding all your eggs around the ground. They've taken some time and planning to procure or create, and now you're letting them go with no guarantee they'll be found again. Even if your egg hunters don't find them, you may well not remember quite where you hid them, either. I'm almost certain you had at least one prickle, scratch, or sting as you poked and prodded them into hiding in the undergrowth. Which of your habits and routines, that you've spent time and energy on, will you place into God's safekeeping this Lent, ready to see if you want to pick them up again later?

> Lord, as I place these things into your safekeeping, I know and trust that you will show me what to take back at the end of Lent, and what to leave behind. Amen.

Journeying on

If you are an egg hider, watch the egg seekers carefully. See how they search low under brambles, in the muddy bit behind the logs, high up in that tangled ivy. Observe how they notice the spiders and the woodlice, and the discarded hazelnut shells from the mice. See how some of them find a sturdy stick to help them hunt, and others get a bit distracted digging a short bit of twig into the soil and watching it crumble. Listen out for the initial frantic rush, the huffs of frustration and the joy of discovery. Watch how you too are a seeker, how you notice the beauty of the world around you, how you rush to search for God's ways, sometimes stumbling, and how you find joy.

> Lord, thank you for the excitement of a life to be lived, of a path to be found, of a kingdom to search for, and that you share in our frustrations and our joy throughout it all.
> Amen.

I SPY SPRING

You could take yourself off for a walk to spot signs of spring and have a nice peaceful time, but sometimes discoveries are no fun with nobody to share them with! Think of a wild place you can get to easily and drag along some people to join you. If you mention that you might be bringing biscuits, you should find some friends appear. Check the weather and make sure that people are wearing sensible clothing. If it's due to rain, go anyway but suggest everyone wears a raincoat and maybe waterproof trousers.

Find a clearing in the middle of your space and put down a couple of waterproof-backed picnic rugs (or choose a place with a nice log to sit on). Give everyone five minutes to go off and find something that shows them spring is coming – buds, new growth, birds building nests, butterflies coming out of hibernation. Remind people just to look, not to pick. Have a good wander over the site, remembering to look under things and high up, as well as just at eye level. You're not necessarily trying to find something flashy, but looking to notice the small changes that show you spring is coming.

When you come back together, pass a talking stick around the group (this is just a stick to show whose turn it is to speak) and tell the others what you've spotted. I wonder if anyone spots something that nobody else does. After a biscuit or two, some members of the group may be very keen to drag you over to see their finds. Enjoy sharing in their joy and pride.

✿ Setting off

Sitting on your rug or your log, before going off searching, you are already scanning around you to work out where to go, to find a likely spot to hunt in. As you get up to go and find the spring, you may have some idea of what you're planning to see, but your mind is open to spot what it will. You have a good idea of where you might be successful in finding the springtime signs, and head towards these, intent on that open-ended purpose. As we set off to follow the path of Jesus, we have some idea of what it will entail, and some idea about where it is wise to search and listen. We also need to make sure that we keep our minds and hearts open to learn what we'll uncover on the way.

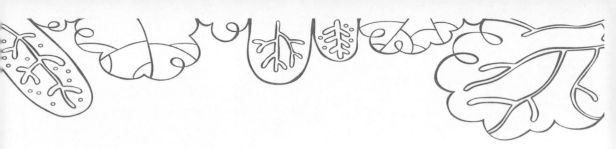

Lord, as I set off, intent on following where
you will lead me, keep my mind and heart open
to what you are going to share with me.
Amen.

Journeying on

Sharing in the discoveries of others makes our own searching more exciting.
Their pride and joy rubs off on us, and looking at what they've found sparks
ideas in us of what to look for and where to find it. It's good, when following
Jesus, to surround ourselves with a wide variety of fellow humans walking
along the same path. The chances are that as they stumble across some
exciting new thought or idea, they'll share it with us, and it'll make our steps
more purposeful and enthusiastic.

Lord, thank you for the joy of other people's
discoveries. Surround me with friends of yours,
to give me joy as I travel your path.
Amen.

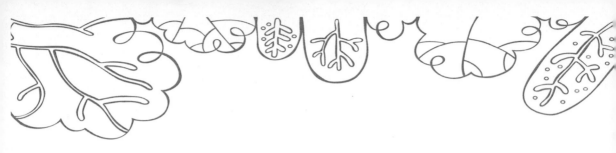

BLINDFOLD SENSORY TRAIL

There are so many textures to springtime, and they can get a bit lost in the visual overload of new leaves zinging in bright yellow-green, and puffs of blossom scattering in the breeze. To focus down and really notice the stickiness of the mud, the roughness of the bark, the waxiness of a petal, the silk of the protective casing around a leaf bud, take your eyes out of the equation for a while.

Find a long length of rope. This is often sold in cheap supermarkets or DIY shops, or given away from sports centres with climbing walls when it becomes past its date to be safe on the rock face. Tie it to a tree, then wind it along an interesting course, past damp patches, and a variety of plants, trees, and rocks if you can. Watch out for low-lying branches, so people don't get poked in the face or caught up by their hair! If you have enough people with you, station someone by each 'interesting thing', ready to act as a sighted guide, so nothing gets missed.

Tie on a blindfold and use the rope to trace you a path to follow. Move slowly; feel with your feet for uneven ground and with your hands along the rope for the next tree. If you have a sighted guide, follow their instructions to feel the 'interesting thing' they are curating for you. Notice how using your sense of touch gives you a different experience of the object, and how hard it is to trust the guides and the rope.

 ## Into the wilderness

It takes some courage to persuade your feet to take steps along a path when you can't see where you're placing them. Even if you've seen where the rope will be taking you before you put on your blindfold, it's disorientating once your eyes are covered. It's hard to trust where to put your feet. And as you walk, you notice every bump and every stump, and you slither down each slope wondering if the ground will level out before you lose your balance. And amongst all this, you are discovering new stuff about things you thought you knew.

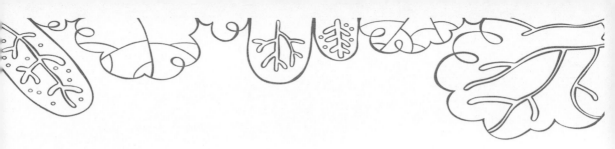

> Lord, help me to trust you through the dark times,
> when I can't see my way, and help me to notice and
> enjoy the things I thought I knew from
> a new perspective.
> Amen.

✿ Finding home

As you take off your blindfold at the end of the trail and look back over the path you've travelled, what was puzzling and confusing at the time becomes clear to you. You can see the trip hazards in context and have to look hard to notice the small and special things you found along the way. But because you did find them, and because you noticed them so closely, you are able to spot them in your journey, even if they look insignificant and instantly forgettable. As we approach the end of Lent, and the end of this Lenten journey, we can look back and see the small and special things we've passed along the way, and can see the part they have played in bringing us to this place.

> Lord, looking back at my journey, I can see so
> many things of beauty to give thanks for. Help me
> to make sure these memories shape my faith for
> the future.
> Amen.

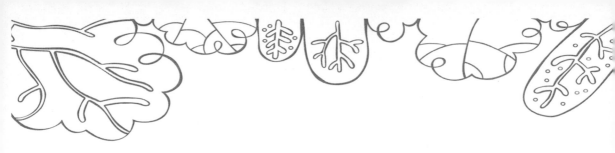

PLAY EAGLE EYE

Here's a game you'll have to collect some other people to play with. You by no means need to include a group of children. We played this and other games when I did Forest School for Grown-Ups this summer, and it was so fun to have a chance to play. So don't get hung up on a silly little thing like age and maturity!

Find a place to play with plenty of hiding places. If it's early in the season, it's going to be trickier to hide, as there'll be less leaf cover, so make sure there are other options, like evergreen bushes, or log piles. One person chooses a base they can touch, where they can see across the whole playing site. As they close their eyes and count to 20 (or 30 if the ground is covered with brambles and ivy), the rest of you go to hide. Now, here's the tricky bit. You have to hide somewhere where you can still see the person back at base, but in a place where you think they won't spot you.

The person back at base finishes counting, and holds up a number of fingers. This is to check that you could still see them – they're at liberty to ask you at the end of the game. The person back at base must always keep part of their body touching the base, although they can move all around it and use their imagination. They peer out, through the hiding places, until they are certain enough to call someone's name. They can add some more details such as the colour of the person's coat and their hiding place. If your name is called, you're out. The last one left hiding becomes the next 'eagle'.

 ## Picking up

This game is excellent practice in being still. Wherever you're hidden, if you can see the 'eagle' then they can definitely see you. If you're still, you'll stay hidden. Even small movements will give you away. The flash of a jacket, a glimpse of your trainers, and the 'eagle' will spot you. Being still isn't something our culture practises or values much, encouraging us to sink our energies into being as busy as possible. But when we're still, there are things we see that otherwise we miss. There are thoughts we can have that

otherwise get crowded out. Taking on the practice of being still is something useful we can do this Lent. As it says in Psalm 46 verse 10, 'Be still and know that I am God'.

> Lord, help me to still myself,
> and to be aware of your presence.
> Amen.

Into the wilderness

When you are the 'eagle', stuck at your base, peering out for signs of other players, it can feel frustrating and lonely. No matter how hard you look, it's as if your companions have deserted you. Sometimes though, you shift your perspective, moving round your base, and something hidden is suddenly revealed. We all have times when we feel frustrated and lonely, abandoned without hope of a solution. These times can overwhelm us and leave us feeling blank or betrayed. Shifting our perspective to try to see clearly from God's point of view can sometimes reveal something new, which can give us hope.

> Lord, when I feel alone and tired
> from searching for solutions,
> give me a new vision
> and a new hope.
> Amen.

NOTES

There are extra pages for your own notes at the end of the book.

SHORT AND EASY THINGS TO MAKE AND DO

Short and easy things to do...

Hapa Zome leaf printing

See
page
68

See
page
70

make a green leafy collage or mosaic

See
page
72

make some elder wood beads

make some bramble string

See page 74

See page 76

make some wild garlic pesto

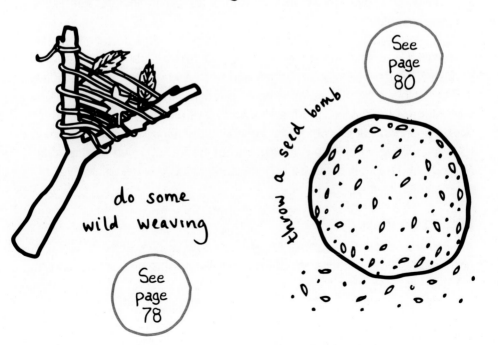

See page 80

throw a seed bomb

do some wild weaving

See page 78

HAPA ZOME

After the grey and brown of winter, it's so exciting when you finally start to see the green appear. First, the shoots are just hints of foliage to come, but before you know it you can see the shapes of leaves in all their variety. Elder is always early to the party, greening up quickly, and after a winter of crumbling leaf litter the tiny bright-green zig-zags around each leaf seem extra precious. As you collect some leaves, you'll notice all that makes them different, so that the canopy springs into sharp focus and you begin to greet new leaves as old friends. 'I know you', you'll think, even if you don't have a name for the leaf yet.

Hapa Zome is the art of making a print from leaves and flowers, using fabric and mallets. Go and have a poke around in your airing cupboard and find that old white sheet you keep meaning to get rid of. Hack it up into pieces – or keep it whole for a huge leaf picture! Maybe cut it into triangles for bunting. Next, you need to go for a leafy wander. Look for nice fresh spring leaves for the best prints and for colour if you can. Dandelions add a splash of yellow (although leave plenty for the bees – they're their first source of nectar in the spring), or you might find a clump of violets or celandine. Use leaves and flowers from your garden or the park – look for interesting shapes and colours.

Once you've collected your leaves and flowers, arrange them on the fabric and cover them with another piece of fabric. (Or fold the fabric over, like a leaf sandwich.) Place it on a hard surface and bash it with a mallet. You'll notice that the colour from the leaves starts to print onto the fabric, along with all the details of their veins and the little fiddly bits around their edges. Once you've pounded out all your latent frustration (!), being very careful to keep your fingers away from the business end of the mallet, open up the fabric, and pick and peel off the squished leaves. This picture won't last forever, but it really captures the beauty.

 Putting down

As you walk around collecting leaves, use it as a chance to do a bit of gardening in your own life. What habits and thoughts are you holding on

to? What beliefs about yourself and your abilities are holding you back from being the person God wants you to be? The familiar seems safe, but it's not always useful to carry everything with us on a journey. We need to take time to sort through it all and carefully put down what we don't need to bring with us. Those things will colour our journey, but not always in the way we expect.

Lord, at the start of my Lent journey, give me the courage to look at what I'm holding, and to place those things that are pulling me down and holding me back into your loving arms, ready to step out and follow where you will lead, unencumbered and free. Amen.

✿ Journeying on

Once you've folded over your leaf sandwich and raised your mallet, enjoy watching the pattern of the leaves appear as you bash. You'll take great satisfaction in following along the stem and veins to find the edges of each leaf. Although you can't see where the leaves are, you have a memory of where you put them, and you know to keep tapping along their lines until you find where they stop. Finding the green from the edge of a leaf rather than just the edge of your bashing is very pleasing! Sometimes our journey takes us on a path that we don't have a map for. Sometimes we have an idea of the route, but have to uncover it little by little on our way. Discovering one part of a path can lead us to find the next bit of the path, and sometimes there is more beauty at the edges than we'd expected.

Lord, following your path doesn't always feel obvious or clear. Help me to trust that you will uncover the path before me, to trust that your way will lead me into beauty, and help me to see that beauty around me. Amen.

STICK A SYMPHONY OF GREEN

Once the leaves start coming, they come in such a variety of shape, size and colour, it makes a huge contrast to the grey-brown days of winter. I like to set a challenge to the children at forest school to collect as many different greens as they can, and they search all around our forest school space.

An easy way to collect leaves, or small bits of leaves, is to prepare a piece of card that you've covered in a couple of lengths of carpet tape. (You can buy this from shops that sell things for the home – it's like extra sticky, extra wide double-sided Sellotape). Experience has shown me it's best to prepare these at home before you head outside; trying to attach the tape onto flapping cardboard without dropping it all in a puddle is far trickier! Once you've reached your place with green leaves – this could be only as far as the garden outside your back door – pull off the paper covering on the tape. (Shove it in your pocket so it doesn't blow away.) Now you have a flat sticky surface to decorate with as many greens as you can manage.

I've seen some very beautiful pieces of stuck-on-leaf art, where pieces of leaf have been torn and arranged almost like a mosaic. I've sometimes seen pictures made, using sticks and other natural materials with the leaves. And even the most haphazard toddler-stuck leaf picture still displays the amazing work the trees and plants are doing all around us, greening up the world.

 **Picking up**

There is much to choose from in this activity – not only which leaves to pick, but also how to arrange them. Should you just pick-and-splat, or should you create a design that means something to you? Should you just use leaves or add in other items to your design? Choosing what you should pick up as a habit or as a practice for this Lent needs to be a choice for you and for you alone. Don't eye up the leaf picture done by your neighbour, but be brave enough to feel your way to your own design.

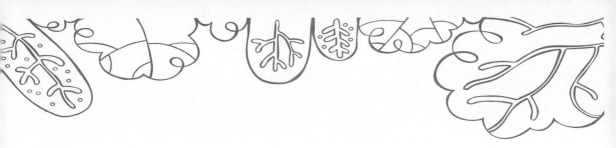

Lord, guide me and prompt me to shape my Lent in the way that will be best for me.
Amen.

Into the wilderness

At first glance, when you stand in a space surrounded by green growing things, they all seem to blend in to one green haze. But, when you're given the task of finding as many different greens as you can, you start to notice other differences, such as how each tree or plant has evolved a slightly different kind of leaf. Even though they're all essentially doing the same job, turning sunlight into energy, each leaf is so specific to the plant it comes from, that you can use them to identify which plant it is. This is also true for us. Our similarities are so much greater than our differences. As humans, we all spend our lives doing essentially the same things (breathing, eating, drinking, moving, thinking, loving, worshipping and praying) but it is in our specifics that Jesus calls us. We are called as ourselves, rather than as some kind of conglomerate human mass. Noticing our similarities can help us to value and celebrate our differences, and follow the path to heaven in our own unique way.

Lord, at times when I feel overwhelmed with the mass of humanity, remind me that you call me as myself to follow you in my own unique way.
Amen.

ELDER WOOD BEADS

In times past our ancestors used to believe that the elder tree was magical. They would thank the elder for his provision as they cut it or picked it. Elders are fantastic trees – they'll grow in any waste ground, and provide armfuls of creamy white flowers in May for elderflower cordial or champagne, and heavy crops of elderberries from late August onwards, which are a great favourite amongst wild creatures.

The other interesting thing about elder is that the wood is filled with a spongey inner. Get some secateurs or loppers and cut off a straight new shoot, one of those ones growing out from the base. If you snip it into lengths of a couple of centimetres each, you'll be able to use a tent peg or a sturdy straight stick to poke through, and the spongey inside will suddenly spring out with a satisfying pop. Be sure to hold only the edges of the elder. Don't grasp it in your fist or you may end up poking the tent peg right through and into your palm. Ouch.

These will be your beads. As the elder is so fresh, you can use a fingernail or a sharp stone to scrape patterns into the bark, or peel the bark off, revealing the bright green wood underneath. Thread them onto string or wool and wear with pride. If you are doing this activity with a pre-schooler, provide them with a couple of pipe cleaners. It's much easier to thread onto something a bit more rigid, and they can twizzle the ends rather than having to pass it back to you to knot.

Setting off

Humans like to take one thing and change it into another. We are tool-using creatures and even something as simple as poking a tent peg through the spongey heart of elder gives us huge satisfaction. Collecting the lengths of elder meant that you could see beyond what they were to what they might become. Choosing to journey with Jesus enables us to see beyond what we are now, with hope to what we might become. We can look beyond our lives with their present obsessions and complications, to what our lives will look like set free and glorious in God's light and love. What tools are you using this Lent?

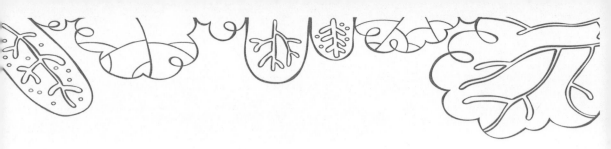

Lord, share with me your vision so I can see beyond what is to what could be, and help me use this time to begin to create something new. Amen.

Into the wilderness

At the beginning, when you poke the tent peg through the length of elder, it can feel like nothing is happening. Depending on how long or how thick your length of elder is, you may find you push, and all your energy does is to compress the spongey insides. Eventually, though, the overwhelming pressure inside the elder wood suddenly causes the spongey bit to give way. Your tent peg leaps out of the end, and the spongey bit goes flying. Sometimes it feels like we are putting so much effort into our prayer life, into reading the Bible, into trying to grow our faith, and yet still nothing seems to be happening. It might be that, like the spongey inside of the elder, our faith too will suddenly leap out, surprising us.

Lord, for those times when it feels like I've hit a wall, when my prayers feel like they're going nowhere, when I feel like I can't get through, remind me that the time will come when things suddenly clear and my faith will glow strongly. Amen.

BRAMBLE CORDAGE

Cordage is the art of turning fibres into a useful cord. It was a skill much valued by our ancestors, who were without the means of nipping to the shop and buying a ball of string, and needed even more than we do now the wherewithal to attach one thing to another. With the new growth in the springtime, there are long lengths of new bramble vines just ready to be turned into cordage. Outdoor experts may disagree on the best time of year to make brambles into cord, but what's surely true is that you can only make cord with the brambles available to you now, so it's worth a go!

Go equipped with a pair of tough leather gardening gloves, so you aren't scratched to pieces. You'll need a pair of secateurs, and maybe a peeler too. And a stout stick. Find a long bramble that is this year's growth – it should have soft spikes that bend or blunt when you push on them and a stem that is soft rather than old and woody. Hold the growing tip with one (gloved) hand and use the stout stick in the other to scrape and bash off all the prickles.

Use the blunt edge of your peeler or a knife to scrape off the darker green bark, revealing the lighter bark underneath. Don't scrape too deep or you'll have scraped through the lighter bark, which is what you are going to use, and only have the woody core left. Once you're holding a length of pale bramble, grasp and twist it, moving your hands along the length of the bramble, to loosen the bark. You'll see that it begins to hang off in thin strips. Gently ease these off the woody core and arrange them together.

If you have a friend with you, get them to hold one end, otherwise stand on it, or tie a small loop and hook it to a branch. Twist and twist the fibres round and round in the same direction until they're tightly twisted. Without letting go, place your finger midway along the length of the bramble fibres, and bring one end to meet the other. You should find that the fibres merrily twist back against themselves, making a strong cord about half the length that the fibres were. This is good strong stuff. You might have something on you that needs tying, and now you can fix it. If not, why not fashion it into a bracelet, awaiting such a time as it might be needed?

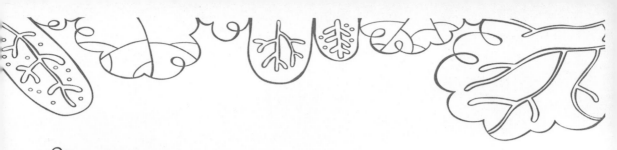

✿ Putting down

Making strong cordage involves a lot of getting rid of the things that we don't need – prickles, outer bark and inner woody core. All of these were useful to the bramble when it was doing the job of busily growing into a tangled web on the ground, but they're not needed if it's to do a job of fixing, carrying or making. What can we strip away from our lives this Lent, leaving just our strong, supple fibres?

> Lord, give me your guidance as I strip away
> the things that aren't necessary for my life
> and for my journey with you.
> Amen.

✿ Journeying on

When you're twizzling those fibres, it begins to feel a little endless. You get cramp in your fingers and every now and again you lose your grip and it frustratingly unravels a bit. It is great fun, though, to watch it twizzle back on itself, and to see the change as the fibres twist in on each other, holding them all in place. As part of following Jesus, we are called to do so as part of a community. There are times when being part of a community feels like a struggle. There's a real fight to keep ourselves part of it, and it can be frustrating when it seems to unravel as fast as we can draw it together. We need to pray for the alchemy that God can provide of binding us together, from all our disparate backgrounds, into one strong cord of love.

> Lord, give me the patience to keep working
> towards living as part of a community of faith,
> and trust that your hands will guide us and
> draw us closer and closer together in your love.
> Amen.

WILD GARLIC PESTO

For my children, the smell of spring is the smell of ransoms, or wild garlic. When they walk along the paths on the Isles of Scilly on holiday, they treat it as a giant self-serve salad bar, and munch their way back to the campsite with green-stained teeth. Wild garlic starts to sprout from early March onwards, green shoots at first, then the white flowers.

Be careful with your plant identification before you eat anything. You shouldn't get wild garlic confused with snowdrops, as although they both have sprays of white bell-like flowers, the snowdrops will be flowering as the wild garlic starts to grow, and will finish flowering well before the wild garlic starts. The most dangerous mistaken identity could be confusing wild garlic with lily of the valley. Lily of the valley has slightly wider leaves, but the best way to be sure that what you've picked really is wild garlic is to break it and smell it. Wild garlic is pungent and sweet, with the unmistakable odour of garlic.

Pick a good handful or two, making sure that you collect them away from the edges of paths where they may have been sprayed by dog wee! Give them a bit of a wash, then chop them finely and bash them in a pestle and mortar, or blitz them in a food processor, along with a little parmesan cheese, a handful of pine nuts, and a couple of tablespoons of oil. Eat it with pasta, or use it on toast, or for dipping.

Picking up

It's interesting identifying plants. When I was asking my children how I could explain what wild garlic was like, so that you could identify it correctly, they found it hard to put in to words. 'It's just wild-garlicky', one of them shrugged. Obviously it's possible to list a plant's characteristics, but the more you get used to finding them, the more you just know which plant is which. With wild garlic, that sweet pungent smell is unmistakable, and once it's passed into your olfactory memory you'll be spotting it everywhere. We need to give things the sniff test to see if they're good for us, and the more we practise, the better we'll get.

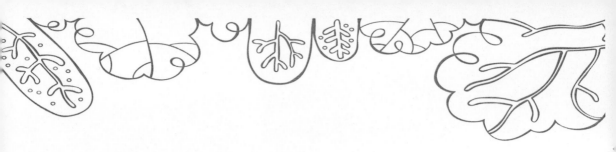

Lord, help me to identify those things that
will be life-giving for me, and to find the time
and discipline to put them into practice.
Amen.

Journeying on

My son was thrilled when he discovered he was walking through a
living larder. Finding wild things to nibble from the hedgerows was great
motivation for a walk. The children will always walk much further, and with
much greater cheerfulness, when there is some kind of wild food they can
snack on as they go. What feeds you, to keep you going on your journey?

Lord, you have surrounded me with good things,
with the wonder and beauty of your creation,
with kindness, thoughtfulness and patience,
with creativity and order. Let me feed on these
good things as I follow you.
Amen.

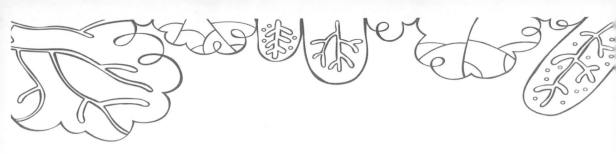

WILD WEAVING

Here's a way you can create something beautiful to bring the budding spring into your home, at least temporarily until it wilts! Find a V-shaped stick, rigid and stiff, not bendy. Tie a length of wool to one of the prongs at the base, then wind it in between the two prongs, taking the wool first around one prong, and then around the other, backwards and forwards, quite close together, until you reach the end of the sticks. Tie the wool at the end so that your warp doesn't start to slip off the sticks.

Forage around to find some things to weave into your wool. There may be fronds of bracken, stalks of cow parsley, feathers, dandelions, cleavers (stickyweed), or strings of ivy. Poke them in and out of your warp, threading them through so that they stay put. If you have more wool in your bag, you might like to alternate woolly weft with weft from natural things. You may choose to create some kind of pattern, or a meaning to your weaving, or simply weave them in as you find them, a visual record of your time outdoors today.

These pieces of woven art won't last forever, so photograph it, and enjoy it while you can.

Setting off

That blank preparation of wool wound around the V-shaped stick is full of expectancy. It's there, just waiting to be transformed, and as you begin to weave in things from the wild space around you, its character changes. The monotonous work of weaving the warp needed to be done to allow the weft to shine. Having put in preparation time for your Lenten journey, enjoy watching it start to take shape and fill out with beauty.

> Lord, I wait in your company, watching
> as you fill my life with love and beauty.
> Amen.

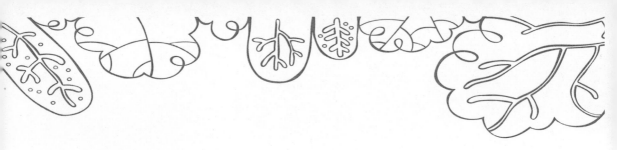

Finding home

If you were to make one of these woven objects in a different setting, it wouldn't turn out the same. Someone could look at yours, and as long as they knew enough about the natural world, would be able to work out in which country it had been made, in which month, and probably which county. They'd be able to see if you'd been near a river or a pond, whether you'd been in a coniferous or a broadleaf woodland, whether your soil was acidic or alkaline. If someone were to look at your life, what might they be able to see? You are unique, called and loved by God.

Lord, as I look over the influences and events of my life, both good and bad, help me to understand that the person they have shaped is the very person you love.
Amen.

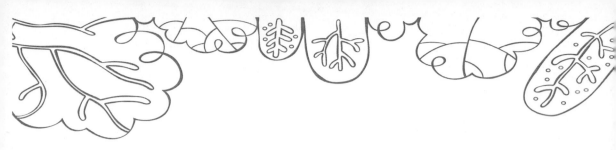

THROW A SEED BOMB

I have a rather fantastic T-shirt that has a print of a tree and some text reading 'Drop seeds not bombs'. Dropping seed bombs is better still, though, and a brilliant way of doing a bit of guerrilla gardening.

First, you need some good clay soil, mixed with enough water to make it malleable and a bit sticky. Grab a small handful of the clay, and squish and roll it into a ball. Next you need a packet of wild flower seeds. Open these up and tip a sprinkle onto the palm of one of your hands. Roll your mud ball around over them – you should find that the sticky wet mud picks them up and they cover the surface of the mud ball. This is your seed bomb. You can make quite a few from one pack of wildflower seed. If it's near the end of Lent, you might consider making egg-shaped clay balls, and storing them in an old egg box, to give to people as alternative Easter eggs.

Take yourself off to somewhere that could do with a bit of brightening up – the scruffy end of your garden, or an unloved flowerbed, a strip of dirt in front of the doctor's surgery or behind the station. Take aim and throw your seed bomb to the ground. The compacted mud should explode, each bit taking a tiny seed or two with it, giving each seed a little bit of a head start and some soil for it to grow in. Not every seed will grow, of course. Remember the parable of the sower! But some will, and the tiny creatures and passing humans will be grateful for them.

❀ Picking up

You hold in your hands a damp muddy ball of potential – potential for beauty. Potential for food to sustain the bees, who pollinate our food sources which in turn sustain us. Potential for the increase in diversity, bringing more insects to the area, and in their turn more birds, bats and small mammals. In all our mess and muddle, we are full of potential. Potential to show God's beauty in the world. Potential to feed and nourish those we encounter. Potential to uncover God's love in all its diversity and for that to bring about change far beyond our reach.

Lord, this muddy ball of clay doesn't look much to me, and yet I know that within it there is abundant life waiting to grow. Help me to see the potential in myself and in others, and to wait expectantly for what will flourish.
Amen.

Finding home

The wildflower seeds in their packet have come from different plants and different places to your palm. As they hurtle through the air to the ground, and the seed bomb explodes, the tiny piece of soil they are attached to will nurture them as they grow, as the root starts to take hold, and as the leaves push up towards the light. The places where we grow may be far distant or very different from the places we began. But our home, God's kingdom, travels with us to wherever we take root, and becomes the strong and fertile soil for us to grow in.

Lord, your love and strength surrounds me wherever I travel.
Amen.

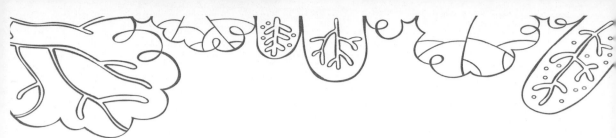

NOTES

There are extra pages for your own notes at the end of the book.

EVEN
SHORTER
AND
EASIER
THINGS
TO DO

Even shorter and easier things to do...

See
page
86

do some cloud watching

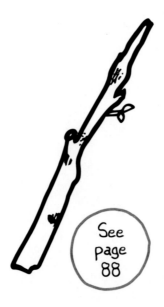

See
page
88

take one stick and
look at it carefully

open your window
and sniff the air!

See
page
90

lift up a brick
or stone to see
who's living underneath!

See
page
92

hug a tree

See
page
94

See
page
96

imagine a bug's journey past pebble boulders
and through grassy jungles

CLOUD WATCHING

I love the sky, how it's always moving and changing. Everyone has access to a little bit of sky and no matter how messy and chaotic our lives can get on the ground, the clouds blow past regardless.

If it's not actually raining, or indeed if you don't mind lying down in the rain, spread out a picnic blanket on the ground outside and spend five minutes looking up. This will save you getting neck ache! If you can't face getting down on the floor, just stand and stare. If you can't leave your home or place of work, grab a cup of tea and look at the sky out of the window for five minutes, or make a date to do some cloud watching from the window of your bus.

Maybe you're having a grey overcast day and can barely see the sun glowing faintly through a layer of altostratus clouds. Perhaps you're fascinated by the wisps of cirrus clouds feathering the blue sky, or are awed by a towering and majestic cumulonimbus heralding the onset of a storm. Clouds are other-worldly and constantly fascinating.

Have a read of Psalm 147:7, 8 while you do your cloud gazing.

Putting down

Cloud watching is one of the most transcendent things I do in my everyday life. Looking up and above helps me to remember that the world is larger than my own fears and concerns. The beauty of the sky helps me to get more of a perspective on my life. That feeling of being absorbed by something so much greater than yourself, with such a different sense of pace and priorities, also reminds me of how it feels to be absorbed into God's reality, putting aside my own timetable and wish lists, and trying to attune myself to the winds of the Holy Spirit.

Lord, as I am filled with a sense of peace and awe watching the clouds above me, so fill me with a sense of peace and awe as I rest in your presence. Amen.

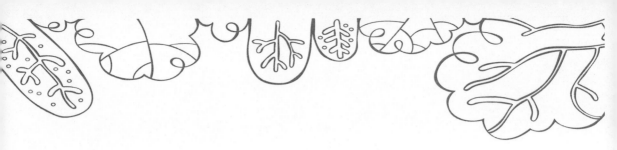

✿ Journeying on

It's amazing to think that those clouds up there are all made out of tiny drops of water, often water as ice crystals, suspended in the air, and shaped and moulded by the air currents and the breeze. Eventually they will fall as rain, soak into the ground and trickle through streams and rivers, maybe even trickle through you! They'll continue their journey possibly as far as the ocean before once more becoming water vapour and soaring up into the skies again. Reflect over your journey in the light of the water cycle. Are there some parts that particularly resonate with you at the moment?

> Lord, as the water you have made speaks to me of my journey, so I am reminded that all your creation gives you praise, and I join in with creation's song. Amen.

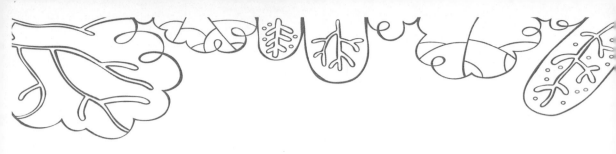

TAKE ONE STICK

Have a look around on the ground and find a stick. There are plenty of sticks under trees, especially if it's been windy or rainy. Choose a stick that you feel drawn to, maybe one that interests you, or feels comfortable in your hand.

Spend a little time getting acquainted with your stick. Is it old or young? How long do you think it spent on the tree before falling to the ground? Does it have lichen on it, or leaf buds? Is it straight or wiggly, or with knobbly bits? Is it rigid or does it bend? If you were to throw it on the ground amongst other sticks, could you find it again?

I wonder what your stick might tell you of the things it saw up there when it was on the tree growing. And what things it saw down on the ground. I wonder where it will end up next.

 ## Journeying on

Looking at the bumps and knobbles on your stick, you can get a good idea of some of the things it has been through in its life. You can see the scars where leaves have grown and then fallen in the autumn. You can see the rough patch where, as it grew, it rubbed against another branch. Maybe you can see a tinge of green on the side that mostly caught the rain, or bumps in the bark from insects moving in. Perhaps your stick reminds you of part of your journey, an emotion or an event. What might your life look like as a stick?

> Lord, reflecting on my journey so far, I know
> that you have walked with me through it all.
> Help me to realise your loving presence
> throughout all my journeying.
> Amen.

 ## Into the wilderness

Your stick was busy growing on the tree until suddenly a gust of wind toppled it and it fell to the ground. It had been part of something huge and grand, something shady, lofty and beautiful, and now all that has gone, left behind

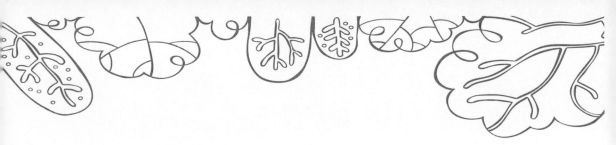

as it fell. But a stick can't be a stick until it falls off its tree. And a stick can do all manner of useful things that a tree cannot. It can be used for poking and prodding, to help a weary walker, and to knock a lost ball out from under the brambles. It can become a pretend fishing rod, a broomstick, a hockey stick. It can be tied with string, or left on the ground to become a hiding place and a home for woodlice and millipedes, and eventually to rot and become more soil to help grow another tree. Sometimes we can suddenly feel rootless and purposeless. But take heart from your stick – maybe there are other things you are being called to do, or to be.

Lord, when it feels as though I've fallen,
and have left my purpose behind, reassure me
that I am being called to be what I am,
as myself, as best as I can.
Amen.

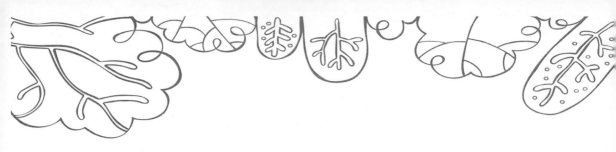

HAVE A GOOD SNIFF

Are you running very short on time today, but would still like some kind of nature connection? Open your door or your window and take a good sniff of the outdoors.

If it's a cold day, let the chill tickle your nose. If it's later in the season, let the warmth carry the scent of blossom to you. When you smell the fragrance of damp air in the spring, you can almost smell the scent of the plants growing. Scientists coined the term 'petrichor' in the 1960s to describe the smell of rain on dry soil. The word comes from an amalgamation of 'petra' meaning rock, and 'ichor', the golden fluid that runs through the veins of gods in Greek mythology. More recently, scientists have discovered that when a raindrop lands on porous soil, it creates an air bubble, which releases aerosols carrying the scents created by bacteria in the soil.

Smells are important to us as humans. They've helped us to locate safe food sources, to find our way and to identify friend and foe. Enjoying the smell of rain may have had an evolutionary purpose as we relied on rain for safe water and for our food to grow.

Picking up

A patch of receptors high in our nose pick up the tiniest amounts of chemicals in the air and translate them into smell in our brains. As the particle of the odour binds to one of the receptors, it triggers an electrical impulse to the brain. Different combinations of these give us different scents. Recently, scientists have estimated that humans can distinguish at least one trillion smells. Like a scent, a tiny thing can have a bigger impact. We don't have to take on huge and difficult things for Lent – doing something small can bring about big changes.

> Lord, you have never been in the business of
> thinking that bigger is better. I remember the story
> of little David being anointed, and of the widow

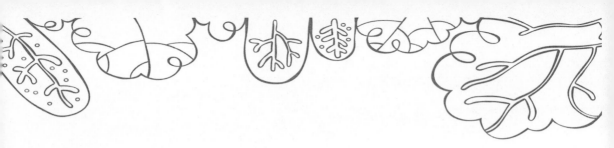

with her mite. Take what I am able to offer you this
Lent, and remind me often that small is beautiful.
Amen.

Finding home

If you close your eyes and smell somewhere familiar to you, you know
exactly where you are. If you were far away and got the scent of your own
garden, your own park, or your own wild space, it would trigger memories
of the place and create a feeling of peace and well-being inside you. What
might the scent of holiness, the smell of our heavenly home be? When do
we catch the odour of it as we go about our lives?

Lord, help me to catch the scent of your holiness
wherever I go.
Amen.

MINI SAFARI

Forget expensive trips to wildlife reserves abroad, there's a whole amazing world waiting for you to enjoy just near where you live. Head outside to your garden if you have one, or a front yard, your local pocket-sized park or a crumbling wall at the edge of the pavement. See if you can find a loose stone or brick, or a big chunk of wood; forget your squeamishness, and ease it up to look underneath. In the damp darkness, you'll be able to see what has made their home there.

You are likely to find some woodlice; did you realise that there are actually 35 species of woodlice in the UK? One of these days, I'm going to go on a proper woodlouse safari and see how many I can tick off my list! They are actually crustaceans, and breathe through their hind legs, which is why they like to hang out in the dampest places they can find. The female woodlouse carries her fertilised eggs underneath her body until they hatch out.

You may well find some slugs hiding in this nice damp place and maybe if you're lucky uncover a clutch of round white eggs. There may be a variety of spiders, and possibly a carefully woven egg sac. You may spot a centipede or millipede as it scuttles off, or a shiny beetle. If you have a wildlife book on your bookshelf, or are able to look them up online, you might want to find out all their names. Or you might just want to enjoy them as they are.

 ## Setting off

I love sharing what's under logs and rocks with the children and their parents who come to my forest school sessions. You never know quite what you'll find. My woodlouse identification is coming along nicely, and I had a small boy recently who commented, 'Oh cute!' when he saw a slug clinging to the underside of the wood. I look around at the anticipatory faces and get a thrill every time. Walking God's path is also an adventure. It's exciting to see where it will lead you. It may well not be exactly where you expect!

Lord, help me to always keep a sense of joyful
anticipation about where you will lead me.
Amen.

Finding home

Looking at animals at home in their habitat helps you make sense of them
better. As you watch a slug managing to squeeze through an impossibly
small hole, or a millipede disappearing down a crack, you understand
why they are the way they are. The woodlice, far from feeling crowded,
actually love being surrounded and hemmed in. Every creature has a
habitat that it thrives within; what is yours? What does your habitat teach
you about who you are? Does the habitat we create in our homes, churches
and communities allow people to feel at home with the God who
created them?

Lord, thank you that you give each of us
a home in you.
Amen.

HUG A TREE

Do you feel grateful for trees? Through photosynthesis, they turn water and carbon dioxide into oxygen. Their leaves and branches shade us from the sun and from rainy downpours. Some produce fruit or nuts for us to eat, or seeds that are fun to play with. They house and shelter hundreds or thousands of creatures. Their roots help to hold the soil together.

Many of the trees around you may well be older than you are. Imagine them curled up inside their seed, waiting to grow, putting down tiny roots. Imagine them surviving the threat of being trodden on or eaten, and patiently growing, year on year. Recent studies seem to show that trees are connected under the soil by fungus mycelium, which enables them to pass on information about threats, and to pass on carbon from a taller, older tree, to a younger smaller one struggling for light underneath the canopy.

It is likely these trees will still be growing here after you have died. For a while, you both inhabit the same place and the same time. Yet you have such a different experience of the world. The tree experiences a world of height and of constant movement while staying fixed in one place. The world changes around it. Visitors come to it. Our vision is set lower, while we travel from place to place, changing the world as much as being changed by it. It doesn't hurt us to sometimes spend a few moments being like a tree – still, and with the world just happening around us. Find a tree and spend some time with it. Touch its bark. Stretch your arms around it. Sit with your back against it. Climb it if it's big enough and you have good enough balance!

❀ Putting down

It is what trees put down that holds them steady. Their root system is as large and complex as the branches overhead. The tree that we can see is only half of the organism. We tend to forget about its roots unless they are poking out of the ground and tripping us up, or if we have to grub out a sapling from the garden. I'm writing this at the edge of Epping Forest,

looking out onto acres of trees as far as I can see, and yet below the ground that's matched by the immensity of their root systems. As well as letting go of things this Lent, what is it you do now that keeps you grounded, keeps you steady and feeds you?

> Lord, let my roots sink deep into you,
> sucking up your life-giving water,
> and holding me firm in your love.
> Amen.

Journeying on

The new research into how trees communicate is fascinating. From being silent and aloof they spring into focus as a community. As the tree's mycelium network warns of threats of disease and supports younger and weaker members by passing along carbon, it reminds us of the communities we are part of. What threads hold us together? How do we support each other and learn from each other?

> Lord, as I travel on my journey with you,
> you build me, and those around me, into a
> community. Help me to work with others,
> to support them and to learn from them.
> Amen.

A BUG'S EYE VIEW

Get down low, and see what the world looks like from a tiny creature's point of view. If the ground is wet or prickly, put down a tarpaulin or a picnic blanket, so you can stretch out full length on the ground, your eyes looking up towards the blades of grass towering above you.

Down here, in the tangle of plant roots and the warm smell of faintly rotting vegetation, is a whole new world that we step over every day. A pebble becomes a boulder. The twig becomes a fallen tree. A feather becomes something magnificent from myth and legend. If you were this tiny, how would you navigate through this place? How would you traverse these obstacles? It's just as well that you'd probably have more legs than you do now! If you were to find yourself suddenly shrinking to this size, where would you make your home?

If you have a few more moments and a length of string or wool (your shoelace will do), find a place to spread it out over the ground. It is less than a metre in our terms. You can probably stride it in one huge step. If this was a path for a tiny creature, what adventures might they have along the way? What tiny wonders would they see? Get down close and look carefully, and imagine.

 ## Journeying on

As you gaze up at the tiny obstacles looming over you, at the beauty around you and the things that surprise you because you've never actually noticed them before from up above; think about your own journey. Sometimes when we are in the middle of something, it all feels too familiar, too close, for us to notice it properly. Take a moment to catch the beauty, notice the challenges and recognise the surprises in your own life.

Lord, help me to notice the life I am in, right now, hidden as it is by familiarity, and to remember that you are here in it with me, as I am in you. Amen.

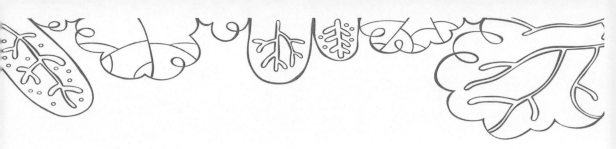

❀ Finding home

Looking over a tiny creature's home, and a tiny creature's path, you can empathise with them and with the challenges and wonders on their journey. You can imagine the effort needed to overcome obstacles and the delight in arriving at a flower and finding its nectar. You stand back up and it all looks so tiny. If you hadn't just been looking at it, you'd barely notice it amongst all the other things in the garden, the park or the forest. What might your life look like to a being far, far greater than you are? Luke 12:7 tells us that even the hairs on our head are counted. All our journeying is held safe within the love of God.

Lord, I give you thanks that my life —
its challenges, its beauty, its wonders,
its pain — is held within your love.
Amen.

NOTES

There are extra pages for your own notes at the end of the book.

THINGS TO DO IN THE EARLY MORNING

Things to do in the early morning...

Open your window at 5am!

See page 102

wash your face in the dew

See page 106

eat your breakfast outside

watch a daisy open

OPEN YOUR WINDOW AT 5AM

I don't know what your sleeping patterns are like. It may be that you do night shift work, so what I am about to share is something you know well already, as you head home in the grey light of dawn and the world is breaking out into a rapturous new day around you. It may be that you have a small baby or an early waking toddler, and little hands grabbing at you at 5am is your new normal wake-up call.

It was when my youngest was tiny and waking me up early, that I decided to make the choice to embrace it, to find something of worth in amongst the yawning and sleep-deprivation headaches. Not every 5am, obviously (I am no saint) but on occasion. Although our house fronted onto a main road in London, we had trees in the garden, and a giant lime and a huge sturdy London plane on the road out front. Some people believe a British spring dawn chorus is one of the wonders of the natural world, and yet here I was sleeping through this marvel every day. I made the decision to open my window and enjoy this spectacle from the comfort of my bed. Hearing the blackbird's song cascading through into my room was magical and (almost) made up for the lack of sleep!

So this exercise doesn't require any special equipment. It doesn't require anything more than a willingness to set your alarm (if you don't have small noisy breathing ones in your house), and ten minutes' worth of wakefulness near an open window, early in the morning. Listen and feel thankful that you are in this time and place, and are fortunate enough to be granted a front-row seat to this natural wonder.

❀ Putting down

I am definitely not a morning person. I love my bed and would happily stay in it until much later than I do! But if I get too comfortable, that sometimes means I miss out. If I cosied up in my bed right through breakfast, I'd miss waving my bigger kids off to school, seeing the castle my younger ones have made from building bricks, and, dare I say, passing more than a brief word with my husband, who is built on a very different body clock!

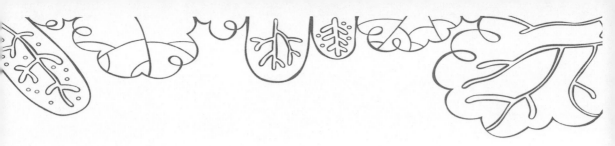

Lent is a good time to step outside our comfort zones to see what other wonders we're missing. And lying in your bed, listening to the dawn chorus is a good wake-up call for us to remember that there are more wonders we have yet to experience. And it reminds us that maybe it's time for us to get a bit uncomfortable and see where God will lead us.

> Lord, I know that sometimes I have made my faith too comfortable. Give me the courage to step outside my comfort zone, and experience the wonders you will show me.
> Amen.

✿ Finding home

My rule number three for forest school is 'Look after forest school'. I make the children stop and listen, to hear who is at home today. Stillness descends on the group and their faces light up as they hear birdsong. I like to tell them how the birds are singing, 'This is my tree! This is my tree!' It is such a beautiful way of making territorial boundaries clear – if only the countries of the world would take note! So what is our territory? Wherever we live, we also belong as citizens of heaven. And just as you've been sleeping through this phenomenon for years, we can sometimes surprise ourselves and notice that we have been living in the heavenly kingdom all along.

> Lord, open our eyes to the beauty of your heavenly kingdom all around us, that we are part of now, in the lives that we live here on earth, as well as after we die.
> Amen.

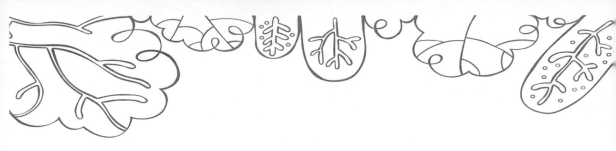

EAT YOUR BREAKFAST OUTSIDE

Later in the year we love going camping. In my opinion, one of the best things about camping is eating your breakfast outside. No matter how much you love being outdoors, living inside a building means you have a lot of day to get through before you even step outside. But in a tent, you get up and immediately head out through the new day to find a toilet. You come back and, well wrapped up, settle down to brew up your morning cup of tea. You sit outside and take your breakfast slowly, soaking up that morning light and those morning sounds. Even by the time your spoon has finished clinking in your bowl, you've been outside longer than you even manage all day, on some days at home.

Why not enjoy the morning by eating your breakfast outside? There's no rule to say you have to eat it holed up behind bricks and mortar. It may be a little chilly, but you can always put on an extra jumper and a coat; and a scarf and hat. It doesn't matter if you look daft. Nobody is looking – they're all eating breakfast inside! Unfold a camping chair or spread out a blanket.

For the easiest, quickest option that won't take any more time from your day, take out your usual cereal or toast and cup of tea. If you've got a tiny bit more time to play with, find a camping gas burner. You could even go for a full camping fry-up, or sit and stir some bubbling porridge. We have been known to make Friday morning before-school pancakes in the garden before now!

✿ Setting off

It's important to eat a good breakfast. Eating well at the beginning of the day is likely to give you more energy as the day goes on, apparently keeps you healthier and helps you stay more alert. Taking your breakfast outside also means you spend more of your day outdoors. There is proof that spending time outside lifts your mood, makes you work more efficiently, and helps you sleep better. And getting a good chunk of time in over breakfast

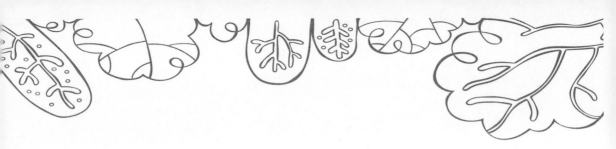

means you're way ahead on this before your day has even properly started! We need to make sure that we keep ourselves well-nourished in our minds, bodies and our souls too.

> Lord, as I fill up on my breakfast and soak up the morning around me outside, fill me also with your peace, hope and joy.
> Amen.

Into the wilderness

Breakfasting outside can be a little inconvenient, especially if you're boiling a camping kettle or cooking your breakfast. Even balancing your bowl of cereal without slopping the milk over the side is a bit of a challenge first thing in the morning. You've got to traipse everything back inside to wash it up, and if you forget your spoon you can't just reach over to the spoon drawer to fetch it. But it does have benefits. Sometimes we end up in difficult situations elsewhere in life, but there may be things we will end up seeing or hearing, learning or doing that we'd have missed otherwise.

> Lord, even when I end up in an unusual or tricky situation, show me what treasure can be found there.
> Amen.

WASH YOUR FACE IN DEW

It's maybe a long way from the first of May yet, but why not give this a go anyway. Traditionally young women would wake up early on May Day to go and wash their faces in the dew. It was said to make them beautiful, keep them looking young, remove freckles or make them lucky in love.

I won't give you any such promises about the dew in your garden or your park. I will suggest that you find a spot well away from dog walkers! Take a flannel and pass it over the grass, so it can soak up the drops of dew. Failing that, soak your hands in the dew so they are wet enough to wash your face with. No matter how sleepy you are this morning, washing your face with refreshing dew, nicely chilled with a bit of a breeze, will wake you up.

You won't find dew every morning. Try a morning after a clear night, so the water vapour evaporating from the ground will have condensed into water droplets thanks to the cooler night air. Or alternatively, you could go outside the morning after a rainy night, and pretend! Depending on how early Lent starts, you may have to substitute dew with frost, which will certainly give you a bit of a zing! Frost is formed in a similar way to dew, just in colder temperatures.

 ## Picking up

Imagine all those young women over the years who have crept out early in the morning to catch the May Day dew. Young women in particular have often had the message given to them that their worth is reflected in their beauty. This is as much true in our times, where indeed all of us are deluged with images of youth and beauty and told that this equals worth and happiness. I wonder how many young women washed with the dew and believed, for a moment, that they were beautiful. As you wash your face, believe and know that you are beautiful. It's not that the dew has magical properties. It's simply that as far as God is concerned, you are indeed a beautiful human.

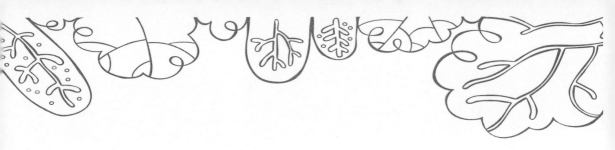

Lord, I sometimes feel overwhelmed with
the message I get given by society and
culture, that I am not good enough as I am.
Remind me that I am indeed a beautiful human,
and help me to pass this knowledge on to others.
Amen.

Finding home

Easter has traditionally been a time for baptisms. In times past, those to
be baptised may have kept vigil through the night, being baptised before
sunrise. An earlier start than the dew-washers, maybe! As you wash with
your dew, remember your baptism and the promises that you made, or
were made on your behalf. These were promises to reject evil and to follow
Christ. Remember too, the promise made to you that God has adopted you
into his family.

Lord, as I prepare for Easter, keep me mindful
of my baptismal promises, and give me joy in
the certainty of your love and welcome.
Amen.

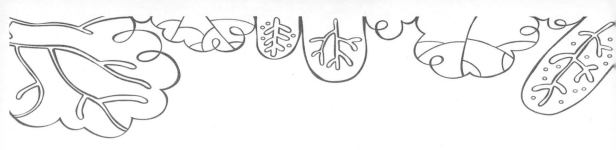

WATCH A DAISY OPEN

Daisies start to flower in lawns from late February onwards, so you're likely to be able to enjoy some daisies this Lent. The name 'daisy' comes from the plant being called the 'day's eye', as they open in the day and close at night. They are actually made up of a mass of tiny flowers within the one flower head, to maximise the number of seeds each can make. The traditional saying goes, 'Spring has not come until you can set your foot upon 12 daisies', and they are such hardy, successful plants that it's not too long after winter until you can do just that.

If you are close enough to a patch of daisies, see if you can sneak up on them while they're still closed for the night. Set up a camping chair, wrap up and sit with a cup of coffee. Make sure you won't be throwing them into shade or you might be waiting longer!

When the sun rises, two proteins are made in the flower, triggering it to open for the day. As the afternoon draws on, the plant destroys those proteins, allowing a third and different protein to be made. Once this is in sufficient quantity, the flower closes for the night. Just before dawn, this third protein is destroyed. The last job it does is to start the plant off making the first two proteins again, and so the dance goes on.

If sitting in the early morning light observing small flowers is impossible today, you can probably find film footage of this phenomenon. Watch the daisy open and unfurl, and then you can also begin your day.

Putting down

The daisy isn't able to make the protein it needs to trigger it opening in the daytime until it has destroyed the protein that shows that it's night-time. As we begin the journey towards our unfurling in the light of Easter, what do we need to destroy that is holding us trapped in the night? As you watch the closed flower, call to mind the things that keep you closed in upon yourself, closed to the warmth of God's love, closed to the needs of others. As the daisy slowly unfurls, offer these to God and imagine yourself opening towards his goodness.

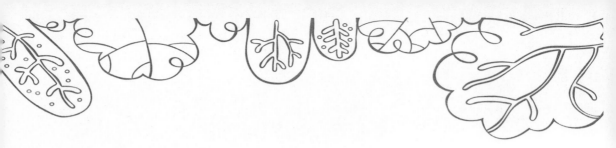

Lord, like the daisy opening to the new day,
I open my life to your goodness.
Amen.

Journeying on

The circadian rhythms of the daisy continue over and over, each and every day. The petals open and close. Its leaves flap. Small pores on the leaf surface open and close. The stalk grows a little bit taller and a little bit taller again. Sometimes that is how it is with our growth. It's not heralded with phenomenal events or lightning bolt moments, but with the gradual day-by-day growing, closer to the person we are called to be.

Lord, help me each day to walk simply and
steadily more closely to you.
Amen.

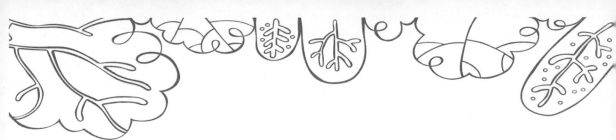

NOTES

There are extra pages for your own notes at the end of the book.

THINGS TO DO ON THE MOVE

Things to do on the move...

See page 114

make a journey stick

go on a barefoot walk

See page 116

go geocaching

See page 118

See page 120

follow a bird's trail...

find your palm tree twin

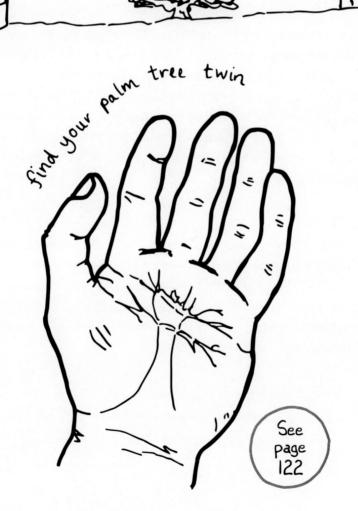

See page 122

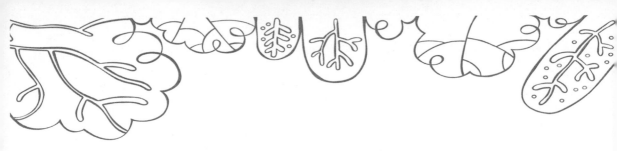

MAKE A JOURNEY STICK

This is one of those simple but very absorbing activities. Bring some lengths of different coloured wool with you on a walk. Each person will need around ten longish lengths of different coloured wool. Where will you go for your walk? If you are pressed for time, you could incorporate it in a walk you would be doing anyway, maybe the school run, or your commute home from the station. If not, your local default 'let's go for a walk' spot is fine.

At the start of the walk, each person involved needs to choose and collect a stick. If it's been windy enough (or you are short enough!) you might manage to collect a stick long enough to act as a walking stick, but any stick will do. Tie a length of wool to the end of your stick, and then as you go, whenever you find something interesting, use the wool to wind it on to your stick as a reminder of your journey. Whenever you change wool, make sure you tie the last bit on, so it doesn't all unravel. At the end of your journey, you will have a multi-coloured stick, holding treasure from all along your way. Looking back along your stick, you are able to retrace your route, remembering everything you passed along the way.

 Putting down

It's impossible to fit everything onto your stick. If you're using your stick as a walking stick, it wouldn't be too functional if it was so bristling with plants and flowers and long strings of ivy that you could barely hold it. You may notice many things on your walk that you will just walk past. Some of the things may have been lovely, but it just wasn't the time or place to collect them. Knowing when to leave things behind is also a skill.

> Lord, if there are things I need to say 'No' to, give
> me the strength and the courage to say so. Remind
> me that I can't do everything, I can't be everything

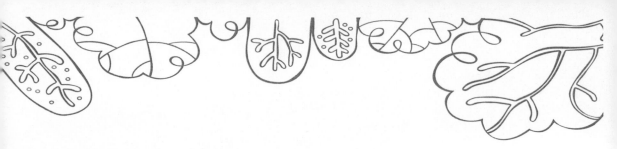

to everyone, and that I don't have to be busier
and busier to be worth everything to you.
Amen.

❁ Journeying on

I wonder what caught your eye as you walked along. Did you find long
grass, or a feather? Did you spot a skeleton leaf, fallen off a tree last autumn?
What about an early spring flower, a sweet-smelling violet or bright
celandine? Your journey stick is unique to your particular journey and from
your particular choices. Our lives are unique, too, thanks to our particular
journey and from our particular choices. The things we choose to carry with
us show our passions and our priorities.

Lord, as I look over what I've collected on my
journey, and what I've chosen to weave into my life
so far, I feel a strong sense of who I am becoming.
Guide me with my choices in the future.
Amen.

BAREFOOT WALK

Shoes are useful things. They keep your feet warm and dry, and protect them from stones and sharp objects. Designers spend millions creating the latest in breathable, well-cushioned stylish comfort. Yet for much of our existence as a species, humans have walked and run around barefoot. Barefoot running is getting more popular. Studies show that children learn better if they're barefoot in the classroom, and having bare feet can help people with neurodiversity to have a better sense of where they are stepping.

Find a path to walk along making sure that it will be free of broken glass and other sharp objects. Take off your shoes and socks and start walking. You'll probably walk more cautiously than normal. That's fine; take your time. Get used to the extra sensory input swirling around your brain. Feel the mud oozing between your toes and the contrast from the crunch of the gravel. Feel the roughness of fallen twigs, the slipperiness of wet leaves, the brush of long grass and the cold shock of a puddle.

Make sure you've brought an old towel so that at the end of the walk you can rub your feet clean and dry, and maybe some old socks to wear on your way home if you like to keep your belongings cleaner than I do!

Into the wilderness

You are placing your feet where they haven't gone before. Normally you protect them from such places but today they are exposed, sometimes painfully, to everything the journey throws at them. If you were to look at an Orthodox icon of Jesus, you may notice that he is always painted with bare feet. This is because the icon is showing you that he walked where you walk. Jesus walked with his feet on our earth, walked a human life like us. There's no place we can place our feet that hasn't already been made holy by his steps.

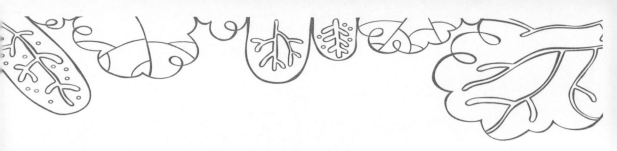

Lord, thank you that no matter how uncomfortable
or difficult the terrain I am walking through,
you have also walked this way.
Walk with me through each step.
Amen.

Finding home

As you sit and rub your feet down at the end of your walk, wiping off
the patches of mud and the grass stains, massaging a little warmth into
your chilled toes, take a while to appreciate your feet. Every day they carry
you thousands of steps. The rough bits and calloused bits just show how
hard they've worked. Remember Jesus acting as a servant, holding and
washing the dirty feet of his disciples. As your feet are probably one of the
least appreciated, hardest-working parts of your body, let them remind
you of the life of service at the heart of the gospel. Home is where you
care for your most grubby and worn-out parts, and where you care for the
tattered and messy bits of other's lives.

Lord, as you washed the feet of your disciples,
help me to notice those who care for me,
and help me to live a life of loving service.
Amen.

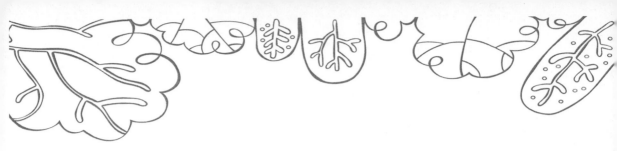

GO GEOCACHING

You don't need much fancy equipment to go geocaching. As long as you can lay your hands on a smartphone and have a little roaming credit, you will be able to download a geocaching app and have a go. Don't worry if you've never done anything like this before. It's all pretty simple. Geocaching is a bit like an electronically assisted treasure hunt.

The app should show some kind of a map or a list of geocaches near you. Choose one that you fancy trying to find. Your GPS system on your phone will guide you to where a small box or container is hidden. It may be that there is a piece of paper inside to write your initials and the date, or there might be enough space to swap a tiny Christmas cracker-sized piece of 'treasure'. Sometimes you will have a series of clues to follow, or there'll be a clue to help you locate the cache.

Once you've found your geocache, check carefully that nobody is watching ('muggles' or non-geocaching folk, in geocache jargon) while you remove it, log your entry, and sneak it back to the place you found it. Make sure you hide it exactly as you found it, so that the next hunters are able to find it. Log your find online too, and read the entries from other recent searchers. If it's somewhere you pass often, you'll have a warm feeling every time you walk past it, knowing that secrets are hidden there.

Picking up

Not only do you now have a new app on your phone, and possibly a small new piece of plastic bling, you've got a new skill and maybe even a new hobby. It's good to keep an open mind and try new things. You might find you like them. Today you learned how to do something new and it paid off – you found the treasure. Or, even if you didn't find the treasure today, you'll know better how to do so next time you find yourself in a geocaching hot spot. People have been coming up with ways to search for spiritual treasure for several thousand years. Try out a new spiritual discipline this Lent: Lectio Divina, praying with prayer beads, using the Jesus prayer, Taizé chants, are just a few suggestions. You might find that they help you search for treasure.

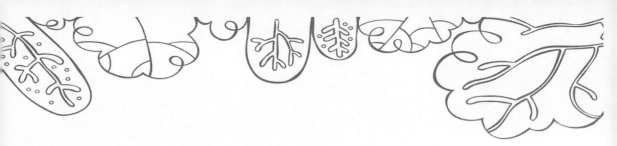

Lord, help me search for the treasure
of your kingdom this Lent.
Amen.

🌸 Setting off

If you've never done geocaching before, the chances are that as you prime your phone and start following its instructions to a destination you're not quite sure of, you'll feel a bit daft as you start walking. It's hard to put your trust in something as out of your control as some satellites in orbit around the earth, and the vagaries of other people's ability to hide a cache where they say they will. Jesus calls us to step out in faith and follow him where he leads us. We may not know exactly where we're going, but we trust that Jesus will lead us to the treasure of heaven.

Lord, give me the faith to follow
where you will lead me.
Amen.

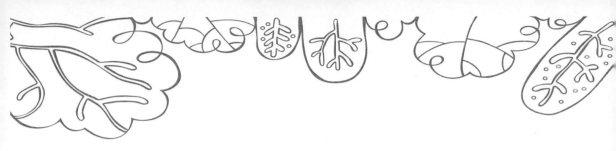

FOLLOW A BIRD'S TRAIL

Often when you're outside, birds will cross your path. They may be flying high up, or hopping around in the undergrowth. Take yourself to a wild space with many paths. Today you will use the birds to choose which path you will take.

Stand at the beginning of your path and keep your eyes open. When you spot a bird, which direction is it moving in? Take that as your cue to start walking. Every time you come to a crossroads, stop once more and find another bird to follow. Let the birds decide for you which path you will take. Make sure you still have some vague idea of where you are, so that once you are ready to head back you won't be completely lost.

Or maybe you could try to follow a bird as far as you can, stealthily creeping behind it, following it from tree to tree. See how far you can get before it leaves you behind. What are your birds up to? Are they looking for food? Are they collecting nesting material? Are they showing off to attract a mate? If there's nobody around to see, perhaps you could try moving like the bird you are following. Try two-foot hopping like the magpie, or striding like a crow, soaring swoops like a swallow or a bouncy undulating path like a goldfinch.

Putting down

We normally make all our own decisions, and make our own choices about how to live. Relinquishing your choices to something as arbitrary as a bird's flight makes a walk different from usual. We like to feel that we are in control of our lives and of our destiny, but the more we see ourselves as part of creation, the more we realise we are all enmeshed in this together. In the baptism service, you or others on your behalf promised to 'submit to Christ'. When we see clearly that our semblance of control is no more than an impression, entrusting our lives to God becomes a joy rather than it becoming a sacrifice.

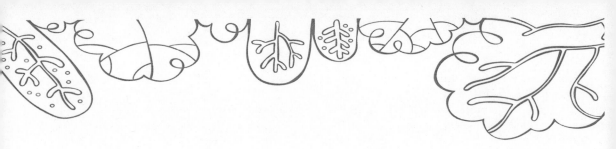

Lord, I trust you with my life, with my hopes
and with my dreams.
Amen.

🌸 Setting off

If you look in a birdwatching book, you will notice that birds can be identified not only by their feathers, or by their size, but also by their flight pattern. The way that they move can help to give information about the kind of birds they are. We move in different ways, too. Some of us dash from one thing to another, getting very excited about each new project or idea. Some of us like to plan and come at things methodically. Some of us are good at sustaining interest in something, and practising it often. Some of us have short attention spans but throw ourselves into whatever we're doing in the present moment wholeheartedly. It is tempting to judge ourselves by how we move through life, but take note from the birds; however they move, they move the way they do because of what they are. No one way of travelling is intrinsically better than another way is, and we will enjoy the journey more if we can relax into our own flight pattern.

Lord, as I follow the flight of the birds,
so help me to follow you in my own way.
Amen.

PALM TREES

'Palm trees?' I hear you say. And yes, I know this is a Lent book, and we're not at Palm Sunday yet. This isn't to do with palm leaves though, but rather the palm of your hand, and particularly the lines on your palms.

Turn your hand over, and have a look at your palm. You can see lines crossing it. Trace just a few, with your eye, your finger, or with a pen if you don't mind having a bit of an inky hand. Can you see that they look a little like the branches of a tree?

Use your palm 'tree' as a guide as you walk along a woodland path. Look at each tree you pass, to see if you can find a tree that matches the 'tree' on your palm. Once you do, go and greet it in some way. You are tree twins, after all. Lay your hand on its bark, give it a hug or decorate it around its trunk with leaves, twigs or flowers.

Isaiah 49:16 tells us that God has written us on the palms of his hands. We grow ever more into the image of God our creator.

❀ Journeying on

With the pattern on our palms clear for you to see, you begin walking amongst the trees. You have a clear idea of what you are looking for and, as you go, you are scanning right and left to try to spot it. This tree nearly fits, but it's missing that branch that should stick out just here. That tree has the branches too close together, and this branch bends round at the wrong angle. You begin to notice the shape of the trees and their branches in a more focused way. Each tree you pass that doesn't fit, though lovely in itself, is another step closer to finding your tree twin.

> Lord, with the pattern of your love clear for me to see in the person of Jesus, help me to keep watching for the patterns of your love in the world. Amen.

Finding home

Your tree twin and you share a common pattern, a tiny thing, but something that gives you a sense of connection and a shared place in the world. Within the community of faith, what is the common pattern that binds you together with the others around you? You may be of different ages, and of different cultures and backgrounds. You may not see eye to eye politically, or you may have wildly varying musical tastes, but the pattern of God's love, running through your lives, brings you together as one.

Lord, you have placed me within a community.
Help me to see beyond the differences to find
that your love brings us together.
Amen.

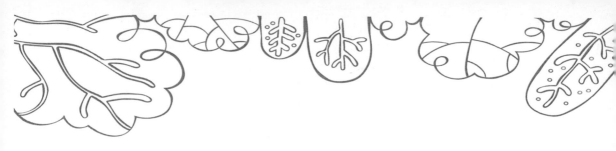

THEMATIC INDEX

Into the wilderness

Finding home

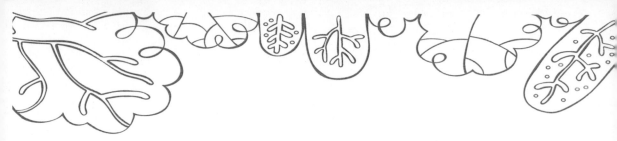

NOTES